OUT

OF

YOUR

MIND

Also by Alan Watts

The Spirit of Zen (1936)

The Legacy of Asia and Western Man (1937)

The Meaning of Happiness (1940)

The Theologica Mystica of St. Dionysius (1944) (translation)

Behold the Spirit (1948)

Easter: Its Story and Meaning (1950)

The Supreme Identity (1950)

The Wisdom of Insecurity (1951)

Myth and Ritual in Christianity (1953)

The Way of Zen (1957)

Nature, Man, and Woman (1958)

"This Is It" and Other Essays on Zen and Spiritual Experience (1960)

Psychotherapy East and West (1961)

The Joyous Cosmology:
Adventures in the Chemistry of Consciousness (1962)

The Two Hands of God: The Myths of Polarity (1963)

Beyond Theology: The Art of Godmanship (1964)

The Book: On the Taboo Against Knowing Who You Are (1966)

Nonsense (1967)

Does It Matter?: Essays on Man's Relation to Materiality (1970)

Erotic Spirituality: The Vision of Konarak (1971)

The Art of Contemplation (1972)

In My Own Way: An Autobiography 1915–1965 (1972)

Cloud-hidden, Whereabouts Unknown: A Mountain Journal (1973)

Posthumous Publications

Tao: The Watercourse Way
(unfinished at the time of his death in 1973, published in 1975)

The Essence of Alan Watts (1974)

Essential Alan Watts (1976)

Uncarved Block, Unbleached Silk: The Mystery of Life (1978)

Om: Creative Meditations (1979)

Play to Live (1982)

Way of Liberation:
Essays and Lectures on the Transformation of the Self (1983)

Out of the Trap (1985)

Diamond Web (1986)

The Early Writings of Alan Watts (1987)

The Modern Mystic: A New Collection of Early Writings (1990)

Talking Zen (1994)

Become Who You Are (1995)

Buddhism: The Religion of No-Religion (1995)

The Philosophies of Asia (1995)

The Tao of Philosophy (1995)

Myth and Religion (1996)

Taoism: Way Beyond Seeking (1997)

Zen and the Beat Way (1997)

Culture of Counterculture (1998)

Eastern Wisdom:
What Is Zen?, What Is Tao?, An Introduction to Meditation (2000)

Eastern Wisdom, Modern Life: Collected Talks: 1960–1969 (2006)

OUT

OF

Tricksters, Interdependence,

YOUR

and the Cosmic Game of

MIND

Hide-and-Seek

Alan Watts

 sounds true
BOULDER, COLORADO

Sounds True
Boulder, CO 80306

Published 2017

Cover design by Jennifer Miles
Book design by Beth Skelley

Source of Recordings:
Alan Watts Electronic University
P.O. Box 2309 San Anselmo, CA USA 94979
email: watts@alanwatts.com
World Wide Web: alanwatts.com

Printed in Canada

Library of Congress Cataloging-in-Publication Data
Names: Watts, Alan, 1915-1973, author.
Title: Out of your mind : tricksters, interdependence, and the cosmic game of
    hide-and-seek / Alan Watts.
Description: Boulder, CO : Sounds True, Inc., 2017.
Identifiers: LCCN 2016034977 (print) | LCCN 2016056050 (ebook) |
    ISBN 9781622037520 (pbk.) | ISBN 9781622037537 (ebook)
Subjects: LCSH: Buddhist philosophy. | Hindu philosophy. | Karma. |
    Spiritual life.
Classification: LCC B162 .W48 2017 (print) | LCC B162 (ebook) |
    DDC 191—dc23
LC record available at https://lccn.loc.gov/2016034977

10 9 8 7 6 5 4 3 2 1

Contents

Acknowledgments

Many thanks to Robert Lee for skillfully crafting these talks into a wonderful book, and to Tami Simon and the entire crew at Sounds True for taking a wonderful collection of lectures and turning them into something truly spectacular over the years in producing and publishing *Out of Your Mind*.

Preface by Mark Watts

Back in the midfifties, my father gained a large following for his public radio talks on station KPFA in Berkeley, California, and these talks were soon followed by the bestselling *Way of Zen* and his groundbreaking *Psychotherapy East and West*. His approach resonated well with open-minded Bay Area audiences as he examined the wisdoms of Asia through the fresh lenses of Western psychology and the emerging scientific revelations of the postatomic age. In his talks, he often suggested that Buddhism should be thought of as a form of psychotherapy, and was not to be compared with Western religions. Instead, he felt that in essence ecological awareness and mystical experience were expressions of the same form of awakened experience. By the early sixties, his radio talks and landmark books had nudged him out onto the college speaking circuit, and for the next twelve years, he delivered large-hall public lectures and more intimate seminars to groups across the country. Many of these sessions were recorded and collected.

Nearly ten years ago, after reviewing dozens of the seminars my father recorded in the late sixties and early seventies, I selected recordings—that flowed together beautifully—from six historic events to become the *Out of Your Mind* audio collection. They are all exceptional sessions, including "The Nature of Consciousness," "Web of Life," "Inevitable Ecstasy," "The World as Just So," "The World as Self," and "The World as Emptiness."

Upon its release, *Out of Your Mind* was an immediate success, and over the years it became one of the most listened-to Alan Watts series of all time, attracting audiences from all over the world.

The series of talks began with all-encompassing themes, including core issues of shared perception, comparative cosmology, and humankind's place in the natural world. In these talks, my father demonstrated convincingly that most of the common sense of the Western world is rooted in outdated science and the dominant cultural constructs of the nineteenth century. Always ready to challenge the status quo, he tackled assumptions that many took for granted, demonstrating how out of touch with the contemporary state of knowledge the "everyday reality" of the Western world had become.

As this body of work developed, he also offered solutions, both psychological and cosmological, and in drawing increasingly from the Buddhist worldview that he explored in these seminars, he offered a fresh and convincing alternative perspective, one of a universe in which we are both inseparable and welcome participants, and at the same time expressions of the "entire works." In this ultimately reciprocal worldview, we find not only our place in and of nature, but also the tools with which to share this mind-shifting perspective of life with others.

Even though I understood the power of these talks, I was unprepared for what began to happen as they made their way out and into the world. In addition to being popular with many of Sounds True's listeners, the collection began to attract a new, younger audience, and several years after its release, quotes and videos began to pop up regularly on social media. Creative video posts based on clips were getting millions of views as well (twenty million at last count), and it is by far the most rewarding aspect of continuing my father's works to see how these ideas are received in the lives of many, and to watch as they take on new forms and continue to grow.

PART ONE

THE NATURE

OF

CONSCIOUSNESS

1

Cosmological Models of the World

I want to start by looking at some of the basic ideas that underlie our common sense in the West—our fundamental notions about what life is all about. There are historical origins for these ideas, and their influence is a lot stronger than most people realize. I'm referring to our essential beliefs about the world—beliefs that are built into our systems of logic and the very nature of the language we use.

I'll use the word *myth* to refer to these ideas. Not to denote something untrue, but to call to mind something quite powerful. A myth in this sense is an image we use to make sense of the world, and at present, we live under the influence of two extremely powerful images, both of which are entirely inadequate in the present state of scientific knowledge. One of our most important challenges today is to replace these myths with an adequate, satisfying, and sensible image of the world that accords with our actual experience of it.

So, the two fundamental images of the world that we've been operating under for more than two thousand years are essentially models of the universe: the *ceramic model* and the *fully automatic model*. Let's look at the first of these, the ceramic model.

The ceramic model of the universe originates from the book of Genesis, from which Judaism, Christianity, and Islam all derive their basic picture of the world. And the image of the world that comes from the book of Genesis is that the world is an artifact made by the

Creator—just as a potter forms pots out of clay, or a carpenter fashions tables and chairs from wood. Don't forget that Jesus, the Son of God, is also the son of a carpenter. So, in this way, the image of God we have is one of a potter, carpenter, technician, or architect who creates the universe in accordance with his plan.

Essential to this first model of the universe is the notion that the world consists of *stuff*—primordial matter or substance. And just as the potter takes clay and imposes his will upon it, so does the Creator craft the universe out of this fundamental stuff. He takes it and makes it into whatever he wants. And so in the book of Genesis, the Lord God makes Adam out of dust—he fashions a clay figurine, breathes into it, and it becomes *alive*. The clay becomes *informed*. See, by itself, the clay is formless and comes with no intelligence, so it requires an external intelligence—an external energy—to bring it to life and put some sense in it.

This is how we've inherited the concept of ourselves as artifacts, as things that were *made*. In our culture, children ask their parents, "How was I made?" or "Who made me?" But these aren't questions asked by Chinese or Indian (specifically, Hindu) children. Now, a Chinese child might ask her mother, "How did I grow?" But *growing* and *making* are entirely different procedures. You see, when you *make* something, you put it together—you arrange its parts, you work from the *out*side to the *in*. Again, that's how a potter works on clay, or a sculptor works on stone. However, when you watch something *grow*, it happens in the opposite direction—that is, from the *in*side to the *out*. *Growth* means that something expands, burgeons, blossoms, and happens all over itself at once. The original, simple form of a living cell in the womb will progressively complicate itself.

That's what the *growing* process looks like, as opposed to the *making* process. Note that in this model, there's a fundamental difference between the *maker* and the *made* thing, between the Creator and his creature.

Where did this idea originate? Basically, the ceramic model of the universe came out of cultures with monarchical forms of government. And so, for them, the maker of the universe was also conceived as the king of the universe—"King of kings, Lord of lords, only Ruler of princes . . ."—I'm quoting from the Book of Common Prayer here. People who orient themselves to the universe in this way relate to basic reality as a subject relates to a king, and so they're on very humble terms with whatever it is that runs the whole show. I find it odd that here in the United States, citizens of a democracy still hold to such a monarchical theory of the universe.

So the idea that we must kneel, bow, and prostrate before the Lord of the universe out of humility and respect is a holdover from ancient Near Eastern cultures. But why? Basically, no one is more frightened than a tyrant. That's why he sits with his back to the wall while you must approach him from below with your face to the ground. See, you can't use your weapons that way. When you approach the ruler, you don't stand up and face him, because you might attack him. And very well you might, because he rules your life, and the man who rules your life is the biggest crook in the bunch. In other words, the ruler is the one who's allowed to commit crimes against you; *criminals* are just people we lock up in jail.

So, when you design a church, what does it look like? Although this has changed in some cases, for the longest time the Catholic Church placed the altar with its back to the wall at the east end of the building. The altar is the throne, and the priest is the chief—the vizier of the court—and he makes obeisance to the throne in front. And all the people face the throne and kneel down before it. A great Catholic cathedral is called a basilica, from the Greek *basileus*, which means "king." So a basilica is the house of the king, and the ritual of the Catholic Church is based on the court rituals of Byzantium. A Protestant church looks a little different—it resembles a judicial court-house—but its appearance betrays a belief in the same model of the universe. The judge in an American court wears a black robe, as did Protestant ministers, and everyone sits in some kind of box—pulpits and pews that resemble where the judge and members of the jury sit.

These forms of Christianity share an autocratic view of the nature of the universe, so the architecture of their churches reflects that view.

The Catholic version builds everything around the *king*, whereas the Protestant church is designed around the *judge*. But when you try to apply these images to the universe itself—to the very nature of life—you find them very limiting.

To begin with, let's look at the supposed split between matter and spirit—an idea essential to the ceramic model. What is *matter*? It's a question that physicists once attempted to explore, because they sought to understand the fundamental substance of the world, but that question—"What is matter?"—is one they stopped asking long ago. See, in exploring the nature of matter, physicists realized they could only describe it in terms of behavior—in terms of form and pattern. In finding smaller and smaller particles—atoms, electrons, protons, all sorts of nuclear particles—you never arrive at any fundamental stuff, so you can only describe how it appears to act.

What happens is this: We use the word *stuff* because that's how the world looks when our eyes are out of focus. We think of stuff as if it were some kind of undifferentiated goo, but that's merely because our vision is fuzzy. When we focus, we're able to see forms and patterns, and all we can really talk about is patterns. The picture of the world offered by the most sophisticated efforts of physics today is not one of formed stuff or potted clay, but patterns—self-moving, self-designing, dancing patterns. But our common sense hasn't yet caught up with this new picture.

And that brings us to our second operating image of the world—the fully automatic model. As Western thought evolved, the ceramic model ran into trouble. For the longest time, Western science was influenced by Judaism, Christianity, and Islam to assume that particular laws of nature existed and that these laws were established in the beginning by the Creator, the maker of the universe. So we have tended to think of all natural phenomena as obeying certain laws according to plan, like a well-behaved machine—a timely streetcar, train, or tram. Well, in the eighteenth century, Western intellectuals began to question this idea, specifically whether or not a prime mover—a universal architect—actually exists. They reasoned that there might be universal laws, but that doesn't necessitate a creator of those laws.

See, the hypothesis of God did little in the way of helping to make predictions, and that's the business of science: *What's going to happen?* By studying the behavior of the past and describing it carefully, we can make predictions about what's going to happen in the future—that's really the whole of science. And to do this and to make successful predictions, it turns out that you don't need God as a hypothesis, because it makes no difference to anything. So they dropped the God hypothesis and kept the hypothesis of law, because you can make predictions from behavioral regularities in the universe. They got rid of the lawmaker and kept the law.

And this is how we arrived at the current conception of the universe as a machine, as something that functions according to clocklike, mechanical principles. Newton's image of the world is based on billiards—atoms are like billiard balls that bang each other around at predictable angles. And the behavior of every individual, therefore, is viewed as a complex arrangement of billiard balls being banged around by everything else. This is the fully automatic model of the universe. The notion of reality as blind energy. We see this in the nineteenth- century thought of Ernst Haeckel and T. H. Huxley, who described the world as nothing but unintelligent force, as well as in the philosophy of Freud, who identified our basic psychological energy as libido—blind lust.

So, according to this view, we're all flukes. Out of the exuberance of blind energy and the result of pure chance, here we are with all our values, languages, cultures, and love. It's like the idea that one thousand monkeys banging away at one thousand typewriters for millions of years will eventually write the *Encyclopedia Britannica* and then immediately relapse into typing nonsense. But if we subscribe to this idea and like being alive and human, we end up needing to fight nature at every turn, because nature will turn us back into nonsense the moment we let it. And so we impose our will upon the world as if it were something completely alien to us—something that exists on the outside. That's why we have a culture based on the idea of war between people and nature.

Additionally, in the United States, we define manliness in terms of aggression. I think it must be because we're frightened. We put on this show of being tough guys, but it's completely unnecessary, you know. If you have what it takes, you don't need to put on an act, and you certainly don't need to beat nature into submission. Why be hostile to nature?

You are not something separate from nature. You are an aspect or a symptom of nature. You, as a human being, grow out of this physical universe in exactly the same way that an apple grows out of an apple tree. A tree that grows apples is a tree with apples, just as a universe in which human beings appear is a universe of human beings. The existence of people is symptomatic of the kind of universe we live in, but under the influence of our two great myths—the ceramic and fully automatic models of the universe—we feel that we do not belong in the world. In popular speech, we say, "I came into the world," but we didn't—we came *out* of the world.

Most people have the sensation that they are a *something* that exists inside a bag of skin. We feel we are a consciousness looking out at this thing. And then we look at others who resemble us and consider them as people as long as they have similar skin color or religion or what-have-you. Note that when we decide to destroy a particular set of people, we always define them as *unpeople*—not exactly human. So we call them monkeys or monsters or machines, but definitely not people. Whatever hostility we carry toward others and the external world comes from this superstition, [this myth,] an absolutely unfounded theory that we're something that only exists inside our own skin.

I want to propose a different idea. Let's start with the big bang, the theory that billions of years ago, there was a primordial explosion that flung all these galaxies and stars into space. Let's just say for the sake of argument that was the way it happened. It's like someone took a bottle of ink and smashed it against a wall—the ink spread from the big splash in the middle, and out on the edges you have all of these fine droplets in complicated patterns. Just like that, there was a big bang at the beginning of things, and it spread out through space, and you and

I are sitting here as complicated human beings way out on the fringes of that initial explosion.

If you think that you are something that exists inside your own skin, you will define yourself as one complicated, tiny curlicue among others out on the edge of space. Maybe billions of years ago, you were part of that big bang, but now you aren't—you're something separate. But it's only because you've cut yourself off; it all depends on how you define yourself. And here's my alternative idea: If there was a big bang at the beginning of time, you are not something that is the *result* of that explosion at the end of the process. You *are* the process.

You are the big bang. You are the original force of the universe manifesting as whoever you are in the moment. You define yourself as Mr. or Mrs. or Ms. So-and-So, but you're actually the primordial energy of the universe that's still in process. It's just that you learned to define yourself as something separate.

This is one of the basic assumptions that follows from the myths we've been taught to believe. We actually think that separate things and separate events exist. I once asked a group of teenagers how they would define a "thing." At first they said, "A thing is an object," but that's just a synonym—just a different word for "thing." But then one smart girl in the group said, "A thing is a noun," and she was right. But a noun isn't part of nature—it's a part of speech. Nouns don't exist in the physical world, and neither do separate things.

See, the physical world is *wiggly*. Clouds, mountains, trees, people—everything is wiggly. It's only when human beings get working on things that they build buildings in straight lines and try to make the world unwiggly. But here we are—sitting in rooms with all these straight lines—but each one of us is wiggly as all get-out.

When you want control over something that wiggles, it's pretty difficult. A fish is extremely wiggly. When you try to grab a fish, it slips right out of your grasp; so how do you get a hold of it? You use a net. In the same way, we use nets to hold on to the wiggly world. If you want to control a wiggle, you've got to throw some kind of net over it. That's our foundation for measuring the world: nets with so many holes across and so many holes up and down to help us determine where each wiggle is in terms of the holes in that net. And this is how we break up wiggles into bits. This part of the wiggle is a thing, this other part of the wiggle is an event, and we talk about the bits as if they were separate things unto themselves. But in nature, wiggles don't come "pre-bitted." That's just our way of measuring and controlling patterns and processes. If you want to eat a chicken, you have to cut it up in order to take a bite—it doesn't come already *bitten*. In the same way, the world doesn't come *thinged*. It doesn't arrive already *evented*.

You and I are as continuous with the physical universe as a wave is continuous with the ocean. The ocean *waves*, the universe *peoples*. But we have been hypnotized—literally hypnotized—into feeling and sensing that we exist as separate entities inside our own skin. We don't identify with the original big bang—we think we are just something out on the end of it. So we're all scared stiff. Because our wave is going to disappear, and we're going to die, and that's going to be just awful. As one priest I know is fond of saying, "We're nothing. But something happens between the maternity ward and the crematorium." And that's the mythology we're operating under. Which is why everyone feels unhappy and miserable.

Some people might claim to be Christians. They might go to church, might say they believe in heaven and the afterlife, but they don't. They just think they *ought* to believe in such and such a way. They just believe they *should* believe in the teachings of Christ, but what they really believe in is the fully automatic model. And most of us believe this way—that we're some kind of cosmic fluke, that we're a separate event occurring between the maternity ward and the crematorium, and lights out—that's it.

Why would anyone think this way? There's no reason to—it isn't even scientific. It's just a myth, a story invented by people who wanted to feel a certain way or play a certain game. See, the game of God became embarrassing. We started with the idea of God as a potter or architect or creator of the universe, and that was good. It made us feel that life was important, that we had meaning, that there was a God who cared. We had a sense of feeling valuable in the eyes of the Father. But after a while, it became embarrassing when we realized that God could see everything we felt and did, right down to our innermost thoughts and feelings. So in order to get rid of that feeling, we became atheists and just started to feel terrible. Because when we got rid of God, we got rid of ourselves. We became nothing but machines.

As Camus put it in *The Myth of Sisyphus*, "There is but one truly serious philosophical problem and that is suicide." And if you believe in the fully automatic model—that you're some kind of separate consciousness existing by yourself out in the blind mechanism of space—then the question of suicide makes a lot of sense. So, whether or not you should commit suicide—that's a good question. Why go on? You should only go on if the game is worth it. The universe has been going on for an incredibly long time, so a satisfactory theory of the universe has to be one worth betting on. That's just common sense. If you want to go on playing the game, you need an optimal theory for playing it, otherwise you might as well commit suicide, because there's no point in the game.

The people who came up with the fully automatic model were playing a funny, sideways kind of game. They said, "All you people who believe in religion are old ladies and wishful thinkers. You want your big daddy up there in the sky to comfort you through the hard times, because life is rough and painful. And the only way you can succeed in life is to bite back and get tough. You have to be strong and face facts. Life is just a bunch of junk, and you have to impose your will on the world and make it do what you want." And this was a convenient theory to come up with when the Europeans were out in the world colonizing natives everywhere. It was a way of justifying their actions and flattering themselves.

Even today, if you're an academic, intelligent person, you're expected to believe in the fully automatic model. No other theory of the world is considered respectable. So, to be an intellectually rigorous person, you're supposed to be prickly.

There are basically two kinds of philosophy: *prickles* and *goo*. Prickly people are precise and logical—they like everything chopped up and clear.

On the other hand, goo people like it vague. In physics, prickly people are those who believe that the ultimate constituency of matter is particles, whereas goo people believe in waves. In philosophy, prickly people are logical positivists, and goo people are idealists. And they're always arguing with each other. But neither could take a position without the other person, because you wouldn't know that you advocated prickles unless there were someone out there advocating goo. You can't know a prickle without the goo. And life is neither prickles nor goo—it's gooey prickles and prickly goo.

I'm a philosopher. If you don't argue with me, I don't know what to think. So if we argue, I have to say "thank you," because owing to the courtesy of your taking a different point of view, I understand what I think and mean. So I can't get rid of you.

But this whole idea that the universe is nothing but unintelligent force playing around out there and not even enjoying it is an incredibly insulting theory of the world. And the people who made that game—the game of putting the world down—thought they were superior because of it. But that just won't do. If you go along with that theory of the world, you become alienated, you feel the world is a mechanism, a trap, and you begin to feel hostile toward it. As if it were a cold arrangement of electronic and neurological mechanisms into which you somehow got caught. And you're stuck in this body that's falling apart, poor thing—you get cancer, the great Siberian Itch, and it's all just terrible. And these mechanic doctors try to help you out, but of course they can't succeed in the end—you're just going to keep falling apart and it's a grim business and it's just too bad. So, in this scenario, if you think that's the way things are, you may as well commit suicide right now.

But maybe you think, after all, that there might be eternal damnation lurking somewhere as a consequence of suicide. Or you think of your children, how they won't have anyone to support them if you kill yourself. So you decide to go on. So you go on in the same frame of mind and teach your children to do the same. And then they go on and support their children without enjoying their lives, and they're afraid to commit suicide too, and so will their children.

So what I'm trying to say here is that the fully automatic model—our basic commonsense notion about the nature of the world that influences most of us in the United States—is simply a myth. The idea is just as phony as the idea of God the Father with a white beard who sits on his throne in heaven. Both are myths. Both come with very little support as being the true state of affairs.

If there is any such thing as intelligence or love or beauty, you find it in other people. Those things exist in human beings, and if they exist in us, it means that intelligence and love and beauty are symptomatic of the scheme of things. Apples are symptomatic of apple trees; roses are symptomatic of rose bushes; and we are symptomatic of the universe. The earth is not some big rock infested with living organisms any more than your skeleton is a series of bones infested with cells. Yes, the earth is geological. But this geological entity grows people, and our lives on earth are symptomatic of a peopling solar system, which in turn is a symptom of our galaxy, and our galaxy is a symptom of a whole company of galaxies, and goodness knows what that's a symptom of.

As a scientist trying to describe the behavior of a living organism, you mostly talk about what a person *does*. In describing who a person *is*, you have to describe what they *do*. And you can't describe what people do inside a vacuum, as if what they do occurs within their own skin. In other words, if you want to talk about a person walking, you have to also describe the floor, because people don't just dangle their legs around in empty space. We move only in relationship. Our actions can be described only within their context. Let's say I'm speaking to you now. My speaking is not a thing unto itself—it requires *you*. I'm speaking to you, and that action is not completely described unless your being here is also described. In order to describe *my* behavior, I have to describe *your* behavior, as well as the behavior of the environment.

So what we have is one big system of behavior, and what I am involves what you are. I don't know who I am unless I know who you are, and you don't know who you are unless you know who I am. A wise rabbi once said, "If I am I because you are you, and you are you because I am I, then I am not I, and you are not you." In other words, we are not separate—we define each other. We depend on each other. If you lean two sticks against each other, and they stand up because they support each other, and you take one stick away, and the other falls down, you clearly see how they interdepend. And this is exactly our situation. We and our environment and all of us together are interdependent systems.

Any good scientist knows that what you call the external world is as much *you* as your own body. Your skin doesn't actually separate you from the world—it's a bridge through which the world flows into you, and you flow into the world. You're just like a whirlpool. The whirlpool has a definite form, but at no time does water stay put in it. The whirlpool is something the stream is *doing*, just as we are things the whole universe is doing. So if I meet you again tomorrow, I'll recognize you as the same whirlpool I saw yesterday, but you're moving. The whole world is moving through you—cosmic rays, oxygen, the stream of steaks and milk and eggs you eat—everything flows right through you. You're a wiggle, and the world is wiggling you.

The problem is we're not taught to feel that way. The myths underlying our culture and underlying our common sense have not taught us to feel identical with the universe. And that's why we feel alien to it, as if we were separate parts confronting the world. But we quite urgently need to feel that we are the eternal universe, each one of us. Otherwise, we're going to keep going crazy, keep destroying the planet, and collectively commit suicide courtesy of nuclear bombs. And that will be that. But maybe there will be life somewhere else in the galaxy. Maybe they'll find a better game.

2

The Dramatic Model

The ceramic model of the world—the world as a political, monarchical state in which we are all here on sufferance as subjects of God and in which we are created artifacts who do not exist in our own right—necessitates profound humility and the need to feel grateful. In this myth, only God exists in his own right. We exist as some kind of favor, and we really *ought* to feel grateful. It's like a stern father who says, "Look at everything I've done for you—all the money I spent on decent clothes and college—and you turn out to be nothing but a hippie, you ungrateful, wretched child!" And you're supposed to be sorry about that and apologize for who you are.

We inherit this idea of a royal God—the King of kings and Lord of lords—from the political structures of Egypt and the Tigris-Euphrates valley. Freud suggested that Amenhotep IV—the pharaoh who abandoned polytheism—is the original author of Moses's monotheism. Jewish law originates from Hammurabi in Babylon. These people lived in cultures where the pyramid and ziggurat clearly indicated a hierarchy of power from the boss all the way down. In the ceramic model, God is the big boss who governs the universe from above.

This is how we've inherited the idea that we govern our own body. We think that the ego—found somewhere in the brain between the ears and eyes—is the governor of our body. And so we can't understand a system of order—a system of life—in which there isn't some kind of governor. But what if there were?

What is this universe? Is it a monarchy? A republic? A mechanism or an organism? If the universe is some kind of mechanism, it follows that it operates by itself (the fully automatic model) or that it's controlled by some great mechanic (the ceramic model). But if the universe is an *organism*, it governs itself, since an organism is a thing that runs itself. In your body, there's no boss. You can argue that the brain is a gadget evolved by the stomach for the purposes of acquiring food. Or you can argue that the stomach is a device evolved by the brain to feed it and keep it alive. Whose game is it—the brain's or the stomach's?

Actually, they're mutual. The brain implies the stomach, the stomach implies the brain, and neither one is boss. Have you heard the story about the fight between different parts of the body and the stomach? The hands, feet, and mouth all turned against the stomach. The hands said, "I work to put food in the mouth." The mouth said, "I chew all this food to put in the stomach." And the feet said, "I walk and walk to carry the hands to get the food it wants." And they all looked at the stomach as this lazy thing that just sat there. So they decided to teach the stomach a lesson. They went on strike. The hands didn't gather food; the mouth didn't chew; and the feet didn't take them anywhere. And pretty soon, they found themselves getting weaker and weaker and weaker because they didn't recognize that it was the stomach's work to feed them.

There's another possibility. Maybe we're part of a system not delineated by the two prevailing myths. Maybe we're not living in a world where we exist as something separate from reality and therefore need to bow down to it and say, "As a great favor, please preserve us in existence." And maybe we're not in a merely mechanical system in which we are nothing but flukes, trapped in the electrical wiring of a nervous system that is, fundamentally, rather inefficiently arranged. So what's the alternative to the ceramic and fully automatic models? What's another image we can use?

I propose the *dramatic image*. Consider the world as a drama. The basis of all drama—of all stories and plots—is the game of hide-and-seek. The first game you play with a baby is hide-and-seek. You put a book in front of your face and peek around at the baby, and the baby starts giggling. The baby understands, because it's close to the origins of life. It comes directly from the womb knowing what everything is all about—it just can't put it into words. Every child psychologist tries to get kids to describe their feelings in psychological jargon, but the baby isn't there yet. It just knows. You put the book in front of your face, you disappear, you peek around, and the baby starts laughing. Because the baby is a recent incarnation of God. The baby knows that hide-and-seek is the basic game.

As children, we were taught our one-two-threes and our ABCs, but we weren't correctly taught the game of black and white. We learned about conflict—black versus white—instead of polarity. The difference is that poles are opposite, but they go together. For example, the poles of a magnet—north and south. What happens if you chop off the north end of a magnet? Well, the remaining magnet will still have north and south poles. You can't get rid of either pole. They may be poles apart, but they go together, and you can't have one without the other. In the same way, we haven't realized that black and white, life and death, good and evil, being and nonbeing, all come from the same center. They imply each other. You can't have one without the other. Self and other go together in the same way as two poles of the same magnet.

When people in our culture slip into a certain state of consciousness and proclaim that they're God, we call these people delusional or insane. It happens to people here and there. In the same way people can catch the flu or measles, you can catch this way of thinking and believe you're God. And when you catch it, your interpretation of the experience all depends on your background. For example, if you think you're the God of popular Christianity—God as king, as the political head of the universe—you might expect omniscient powers and tell everyone to bow down and worship you. But if you live in a Hindu culture and suddenly tell your friends, "Hey, I'm God!" they won't denounce you as insane as much as they'll congratulate you. "Congrats! You finally found out!" Because the Hindu idea of God is not autocratic. Shiva has ten arms. How do you use ten arms? It's hard enough to use two. Try playing the organ—you need both hands for the keys, both feet for the pedals, and you have to play all these different rhythms. It's tricky.

But, actually, we're masters at this. How do you grow each hair? How do you beat your heart? How do you digest your food? And how do you do all this without thinking about it? In your very body, you are omnipotent in the truest sense of the word. You are able to do an infinite number of necessary tasks without giving them the slightest thought.

When I was a child, like most children I regularly asked my mother all sorts of ridiculous questions. Eventually, she got bored with answering and would respond, "Darling, there are some things we're just not meant to know." And I'd ask, "Will we *ever* know?" "Of course," she said. "When we die and go to heaven, God will explain everything to us." So I imagined that in heaven—particularly on wet afternoons—we'd all sit around the throne of Grace and ask questions. "Heavenly Father, why are leaves green?" And he'd say, "Chlorophyll." And we'd say, "Oh."

But in the Hindu universe, if you were to ask God why he made the mountains, he'd just say, "Well, I just did it." And he'd say that because there are no words to describe how the mountains were made. Words can't communicate how mountains are made any more than you can drink the ocean with a fork. A fork is useful for sticking into a piece of meat and eating it, but it won't do for imbibing the ocean. You could do it, but it would take millions of years, and you'd get thoroughly bored. Just as you'd get bored of a description of mountain building, because the mountains weren't built with words. It just happened. Just like you can close and open your hand. How would you use words to explain that? How would you describe how you're able to be conscious? Or beat your own heart? You probably can't put it into words, but you can certainly do it.

So here's our game. We think the only things we truly know are those we can put into words. Let's suppose I fall head over heels for some young woman, and my friend asks, "But do you really love her?" How would I prove that? If I'm articulate—say, I'm a poet—I'd use the language of poetry to convince everyone of the depth of my feelings. Or maybe I'd craft the most beautiful love letters ever written. My friend reads those and says, "Okay—I'm convinced. You really do love her." But what if I'm not articulate? What if I can't describe my feelings very well? I'll have a much harder time convincing others.

Our culture plays a very convincing game that nothing really happens unless it shows up in the newspaper. Our children have started to feel like they don't exist authentically unless they get their names in the papers. And the fastest way to do that is to commit a crime. Then you get photographed, appear in court, and everyone notices you. It only happens if it's recorded. If you shout, and you don't hear an echo, it seems like the shout didn't happen, and that's a real hang-up we have. We like to hear echoes—singing in the shower where there's more resonance, for example. Or playing a musical instrument that has a built-in resonator, like a cello or violin. In the same way, when we're happy, the cortex of the human brain tells us we're happy, and that provides a certain resonance. If you're happy and you don't know it, what's the use?

But herein lies the problem. Several thousand years ago, human beings evolved a system of self-consciousness, and we came to know that we know. At that point in our evolution, we stopped trusting our instincts. Instead, we had to think about everything and discipline our lives according to foresight, words, symbols, calculations, and so on. And then we began to worry. Once you start thinking about things, you worry as to whether you thought enough. Did you really take all the details into consideration? Was every fact properly reviewed? And the more you think about it, the more you realize that you really couldn't take everything into consideration, because all the variables in any human decision are incalculable. So you become anxious. This is the price you pay for knowing that you know, for being able to think about thinking, and feel about feeling. So you're in this funny position.

This reflexive consciousness can be a great advantage, but the downside is terrible. We are aware of reality and have symbols that represent reality; we have wealth and money that represent a kind of wealth. But if you don't realize that the symbol is secondary, it doesn't have the same value. It's like when we go to the supermarket, gather a cartload of goodies, and roll up to the cashier. He says, "That'll be seventy-five dollars, please," and we get depressed, because we don't recognize that we just traded seventy-five dollars' worth of symbolic paper for an actual cartload of goodies. We just think we lost seventy-five dollars. See, the real wealth is in the cart, but we're depressed because, in our system, the symbol has become more valuable than the reality. Money represents power and potentiality, whereas wealth—well, we just think that the food is something that's ordinary and necessary because we have to eat. And that's really mixed up.

But if you awaken from the illusion and understand that black implies white, self implies other, life implies death (or, rather, death implies life), you can begin to feel *yourself*. You can feel that you're not just a stranger in the world, that you're not something here on probation, that you're not fundamentally some sort of fluke, and you can begin to feel your own existence as absolutely fundamental. What you are basically—deep, deep down and far, far in—is simply the fabric and structure of existence itself.

Hindu mythology refers to the world as the drama of God. To Hindus, God is not an old man with a white beard who sits on a throne with royal prerogatives. God is the self, Satchitananda. *Sat* means "that which is," *chit* means "consciousness," and *ananda* means "bliss." The ultimate, unchanging reality is gorgeous, full, and joyful. Just look at the night sky—all those stars are like a fireworks display on the Fourth of July. Just like that, the universe is a celebration.

Let's suppose that you were able to dream any dream you wanted to dream, and that you had the power in one night to dream over one hundred years of your life, or whatever length of time you wished.

Naturally, as you began this adventure of dreams, you'd fulfill all your wishes—you could enjoy every kind of pleasure imaginable. After a hundred years of this type of total pleasure, you might think, "Whoa, that was pretty great, but how about now I have a surprise—let's have a dream that's not under my total control." And so you would. And you would enjoy whatever close shave your mind created for you, and you'd get more and more adventurous, and gamble more and more, and finally you'd dream the very life you're having right now. Within your infinite multiplicity of choices, you'd dream that you were this particular life—you'd dream that you weren't God.

According to this idea, that's the whole nature of God. To play that he's not God. God abandons himself—he gives himself away and gets lost. In this way, everybody is the fundamental reality—not God in a politically kingly sense, but God in the sense of being the self. Deep down, you're all this basic reality, but you're pretending that you're not. And it's perfectly okay to play this game, to pretend that you're not God, because that's the whole notion of drama. You go to the theater and assume your seats to see a comedy, tragedy, thriller, or what-have-you, and you all know that whatever you see on the stage is not for real. But the actors conspire against you. They're going to try to persuade you that what is happening on the stage *is* for real. They want everyone sitting on the edge of their seats. They want you terrified or crying or laughing—absolutely captivated by the drama. And if a skillful human actor can take in an audience and make people cry, just think what a cosmic actor could do. She could take herself in completely and play with so much reality that she would start to really believe in the game.

You're sitting there, really thinking you're *there*. You've persuaded yourself so well. You've acted so well that you just *know* that this is the real world. But you're merely playing. Because the audience and the actor are one.

You know that the word *person* means "mask"? The *persona* was the mask worn by actors in Greek and Roman drama. The mask had a megaphone-type mouth to throw the sound out into an open-air theater. *Per* means "through," and *sona* means "what the sound comes through." That's the mask. How to be a "real" person, how to be a genuine fake—a mask. The *dramatis personae* at the beginning of a play is the list of masks that the actors will wear. In the course of forgetting that this life is a drama, the word for the role—the word for the mask—has come to mean who you *are* genuinely. That is, the person.

I'm not trying to sell you on this idea in the sense of converting you to it. I just want you to play with it. I'm not trying to prove it—I'm just putting it forward as a possibility of life to think about.

Instead of thinking that you're a victim of a mechanical world or an autocratic God, try this on—the life you're living is what *you* have put yourself into. Only you won't admit it because you want to play the game that it *has* happened to you. But instead of blaming your father for getting horny for your mother, and expecting both of them to take responsibility for your crummy life since they brought you into the world, try considering that you were the shiny gleam in your father's eye when he approached your mother, and that it was your intention that led you to become deliberately involved in this particular existence. And even if you've had a terrible life—rife with syphilis and tuberculosis and the Siberian Itch—it has all, nevertheless, been a game. And isn't that an optimal hypothesis?

Look, if you play life on the supposition that you're a helpless little puppet or that life is a frightful, serious risk, it will be an invariable drag. There's no point in going on living unless you make the assumption that the situation of life is optimal, that—really and truly—we're all in a state of total bliss and delight, but we're all pretending otherwise, just for kicks. You play "non bliss" in order to really experience "bliss." And you can really go as far out into the non bliss game as you want, because when you wake up from the game, it'll be great. You can't know black unless you know white, and you can't know white without knowing black. This is simply fundamental.

That's the drama. So, to be frank and sum up my metaphysics: there's the central self—you can call it God or whatever you like—and it's all of us. And it's playing all the parts of every single being throughout the universe, and it's playing the game of hide-and-seek with itself. It gets involved in far-out adventures, it gets lost, but in the end, it always wakes up and comes back to itself. And when you're ready to wake up, you're going to wake up. And if you're not ready to wake up yet, you'll keep pretending that you're just some "poor little me."

But since you're reading this and engaging in some sort of inquiry, I assume that you're in the process of waking up. Or maybe you're just teasing yourself with some kind of flirtation with waking up, which you're not serious about. Or maybe you're not serious, but you're *sincere*—you are ready to wake up. If that's the case—if you really are on the path of waking up, of finding out who you truly are—then you'll meet a character called the *guru*.

To the Hindus, the guru is the teacher, the *awakener*. It's the guru's job to look you in the eye and say, "Oh, come off it—I know who you *really* are!" So whatever you bring to the guru—your problems, your desire to get one up on the universe, your search for enlightenment, your pining for spiritual wisdom, or what-have-you—the guru just looks at you and asks, "Who are you?" People used to approach the famous guru Sri Ramana Maharshi and ask him who they were in their previous incarnations—as if that mattered—and he would look at them and ask, "Who is asking the question?" He'd just say something like, "You're looking at me. You're looking out, but you're unaware of what's behind your own eyes. Go back in and find out who you are." I have a gorgeous photograph of him in my house, and every time I walk past it, I look into his eyes and see the humor in them. I hear his lilting laugh that says, "Oh, come off it! I recognize you, Shiva. What funny clothes you are wearing today!"

Gurus are tricksters, of course. Gurus play all sorts of tricks. And the tricks are meant to put you through the mill, because you won't wake up until you feel you've paid a price for it.

Your deep sense of guilt or anxiety is simply a way of keeping the game going, of continuing to wear your mask, your disguise. Christianity is really good at making you feel guilty for existing.

And you buy into this notion that your very existence is an affront, that you are a fallen human being. When I was a child, during services on Good Friday, they would give each of us a colored postcard with a crucified Jesus on it. And beneath him were the words: *This have I done for thee. What doest thou for me?* And we felt awful! Like we ourselves had nailed Jesus to the cross. And we felt guilty for even daring to exist at all.

But that guilt is a veil across the sanctuary. It's a barrier with a warning sign that says, "Don't you *dare* come in!" When you're going to be initiated on one path or another, before learning the great mystery, there's always someone wiser or more official than you saying, "Nope. Not yet. You have to fulfill this requirement, then that requirement, and then another, and *then* we'll let you in." That's a way of putting you through the mill. Because you won't wake up unless you feel you deserve it, and you won't feel that unless the path is difficult. So you put yourself through one test and another and another until the journey has been sufficiently arduous, and only *then* will you admit to yourself who you really are. That's rather funny, when you think about it.

In Zen, they say that when you attain *satori*, or enlightenment, the only thing left to do is have a good laugh. But Zen masters—every kind of master, for that matter—put up the barrier and run you through the mill, because they're simply playing your own game. Another Zen saying has it that whoever wants to study Zen should be beaten with a stick, because he or she was stupid enough to pretend that they had a problem in the first place. But you don't *have* a problem. *You* are the problem. You put yourself in this situation.

Here's a fundamental question to explore: Do you see yourself as a victim of the world, or do you see yourself *as* the world? If you define yourself merely as the voluntary network of your nervous system, then you've defined yourself as a victim in the game. And so you feel that life is some kind of trap imposed on you by God or fate or the cosmic mechanism, and you can live out your life as some *poor little me.* On the other hand, you could also include in your definition of yourself that which you do involuntarily. You define yourself as the whole works—you beat your own heart, you grow your own hair—and no one imposes this upon you. You're not a victim. *You* are doing it. You might not be able to explain *how* you do it, because it would take too long, and words are boring and clumsy. Regardless, you can claim your life and proclaim with gusto, "I'm responsible." Whether comedy or tragedy, *you* did it.

This seems a better basis for going on. It's fundamentally more joyous and profitable and interesting. And it's a lot better than defining ourselves as miserable victims, sinners, or what-have-you.

3

The Eternal Transaction

So, in the dramatic myth, life as we experience it is a big act, and behind the big act is the player. And the player is the self, the *atman* in Hindu philosophy. That's you. Only you are playing hide-and-seek, but you won't admit it, because you have deliberately forgotten who you really are, which is the foundation of the universe, or the "ground of being" as twentieth-century theologian Paul Tillich calls it. Well, you might remember who you really are somewhere back there or somewhere deep, deep down, but you still can't admit it. So, to bring this knowledge to the front, you have to be kidded out of your game.

We define some actions as voluntary, and we feel in control of those. And then there are those things we consider involuntary. But the dividing line between the two is very arbitrary. For example, moving your hand. When you move your hand, you feel that you decide whether to open or close it, but how do you decide? And before you decide, do you decide to decide? No, you just decide to open your hand. But how do you do that? And if you don't know how you do that, is the action voluntary or involuntary? Or take breathing as another example. You can control your breath, but when you don't think about it, you keep on breathing. So is breath voluntary, involuntary, both? It's arbitrary.

Similarly, we have an arbitrary definition of the self. We think of the self as something with volition, defined by actions we *do*, but that doesn't include such essential functions as breathing (most of the time), our heartbeat, the activity of the glands, digestions, circulation, growing bones, and so on. Even so, you *do* those things, don't you? Of course. And when you get with yourself and find out that you are all these processes, a strange thing begins to happen—you discover that you are one with the universe. The "involuntary" circulation of your blood is one continuous process with the shining stars. And if you find out that you are circulating your blood, you will also discover that you are shining the stars, because your physical organism is one continuous process with everything else going on. Waves are continuous with the ocean. Your body is continuous with the total energy system of the cosmos. It's all you. But you're playing the game that you're just this tiny, little bit of everything.

Omnipotence doesn't mean you know *how* everything is done—it's just doing it. You don't have to be able to translate it into language. Look, suppose when you got up in the morning, you had to switch your brain on, and you had to wake up every single system of your body and activate all the circuits necessary for life. Your day would never get started. All those things need to be happening at once. How does a centipede control a hundred legs at once? It doesn't. They just move—the centipede doesn't have to think about it.

In the same way, you unconsciously perform all the various activities of your organism. Only, *unconsciously* isn't the right word—that sounds sort of dead. *Superconsciously* is a better choice. And what is consciousness? It's simply a specialized form of awareness. When you look around the room, you are conscious only of those details you notice, but you see far more than you notice, because you don't focus your attention on every little object. Similarly, you don't focus your attention on the minute operations of your thyroid gland, and you don't focus your attention on how you make the sun shine.

Let's connect this with the problem of birth and death. A lot of people are afraid that when they die, they're going to have to put up with everlasting nonexistence, but that's not actually an experience. When I was a child, I often imagined what it would be like to go to sleep and never wake up. But if you think about that long enough, another question will come to you. That is, what was it like to wake up after having never gone to sleep? I mean, what was it like to wake up when you were born? See, you can't have the experience of nothing, so after you're dead, the only thing that can happen is the same experience that happened when you were born.

After people die, other people are born, and they're all you. It's just that you can only experience one life at a time. Wherever beings exist throughout all the galaxies, you are all of them—when they come into being, that's *you* coming into being. You don't remember the past in the same way that you don't have to think about how to make your thyroid work. You don't have to know how to shine the sun, you just do it, just as you breathe without thinking about it. Doesn't this astonish you? That you're this fantastically complex thing, that you're performing all these seemingly impossible functions without any education in how to do it? You're a miracle.

The point is that from a strictly physical, scientific standpoint, this organism is a continuous energy with everything else that's going on. If I am my foot, I am the sun. And yet we persist with our little, partial view: "No, I'm just something *in* this body. I'm just this ego." What a joke. The ego is nothing other than the focus of conscious attention. It's like radar on a ship—it's a troubleshooter. Conscious attention is a designed function of the brain to scan the environment for trouble. And if you identify yourself as the troubleshooter, you define yourself as living in a perpetual state of anxiety.

The moment you cease to identify with the ego and become aware that you are the whole organism, you realize how harmonious it all is. Your organism is a miracle of harmony. All these things functioning together—even miniscule creatures fighting each other in your bloodstream and eating each other up. If they weren't doing that, you wouldn't be healthy. What appears to be discord on one level is harmony at a higher level. All the discord in your life and in the lives of others—at a higher level of the universe, all of that is healthy and harmonious. Everything you are and do at that higher level is magnificent and free of blemish, just like patterns in waves, markings in marble, or the rippling movements of a cat. The world is really okay, and it couldn't be anything else. Otherwise, it couldn't exist.

Physical and *spiritual* are out-of-date categories. It's all a process. There isn't *stuff* on one hand and *form* on the other—it's just *pattern*. Life is pattern; it's a dance of energy. I don't claim to have any private revelations about this. I don't have any mystical knowledge about any higher vibratory plane. All this is standing right in front of you. It's just a question of how you look at it.

When you realize this, the most extraordinary thing happens. Some people will use the symbolism of God as a brilliant light, only somehow veiled, hiding underneath all the forms you see. But the truth is actually funnier than that—you're looking at the brilliant light right now. The experience you're having right now—which you might call ordinary, everyday consciousness—is *it*. And when you find that out, you laugh yourself silly. That's the great discovery.

In other words, when you really start to see things and you look at an old paper cup, you realize that old paper cup is the brilliant light of the cosmos. Nothing could be brighter—ten thousand suns couldn't be brighter. It's just that all the points of infinite light are tiny when you see them in the cup, so they don't blow your eyes out. Actually, the source of light is in the eye. If there were no eyes to see the world, the sun would not be light. You evoke light out of the universe in the same way you evoke hardness out of wood by virtue of having soft skin. Wood is only hard in relation to soft skin. Your eardrum evokes sound out of the air. This is how you call into being the whole universe—light, color, hardness, heaviness, everything.

But we've sold ourselves a different mythology. When people began to discover how big the universe actually is, they conceived the idea that we live on this little planet in a solar system on the edge of a galaxy—a minor galaxy—and they thought, "Ah, well—we really are unimportant after all. God isn't there and he doesn't love us and nature doesn't give a damn." And we put ourselves down with that mythology. Whereas, in actuality, it's us—this funny little creature crawling on this planet way out in space somewhere who has the ingenuity by nature of this magnificent organic structure to evoke the universe out of what would otherwise be mere quanta. This little ingenious organism on this planet is what the whole show is growing so that it can realize its own presence.

What do we do with that knowledge? If that's the state of affairs—which it is—the conscious state you're in at this very moment is identical to the divine state. And if you do anything to make that state different, it shows you don't understand that it is so. The moment you start practicing yoga or prayer or meditation or indulging in any sort of spiritual cultivation, you get in your own way.

The Buddha said that we suffer because we desire, so if we can give up desire, we won't suffer. But that isn't the last word. That was merely the opening to a greater dialogue. See, if you tell someone to get rid of desire, all they end up doing is desiring not to desire. You can't give up desire. It's like telling someone to be unselfish or get rid of their ego or let go and relax. Why would you want to do all that? Only because you're trying to beat the game. Because you're still operating under the hypothesis that you are different from the universe, so you want to get one up on it. And competing with the universe just reveals that you don't understand that you *are* the universe. You still think there's a real difference between self and other, but the two are mutually necessary, just like the poles on a magnet.

The guru wants to get this across to you. However, since you're operating under an absurd hypothesis, the guru has to work with that, so he or she runs you through the mill in order to get you to be even more ridiculous, hard, and assiduous than usual. If you put yourself in a contest with the universe, the guru will stir up that contest until it becomes ridiculous. That's why the great teachers give tasks like "abandon your ego" or "thou shalt love the Lord thy God." Well, that puts you in a double blind. You can't love on purpose. You can't be purposely sincere. It's like trying to not think of an elephant.

Christianity is rigged this way. We're told to feel very sorry for our sins, but we all know that we're not. We *think* we *ought* to feel sorry, so we try to be penitent or try to be humble. And the more assiduously we practice, the phonier the whole thing gets. It's the technique of *reductio ad absurdum*. If you think you have a problem—that you're this troubled little ego—a Zen master will say, "Show me. I want to see this ego thing that is such a problem." When Bodhidharma went to China, a disciple approached him and said, "I have no peace of mind. Please help me pacify my mind." And Bodhidharma said, "Okay. Let me see this mind. Bring it to me, and I'll pacify it." And the flummoxed student replied, "I can't. When I look for it, I can't find it." And Bodhidharma said, "There. It's pacified."

When you look for your own mind—that is to say, your own particularized center of being that is separate from everything else—you won't be able to find it. But the only way you'll know it isn't there is if you look for it hard enough to find out that it isn't there. That's why gurus of all types tell you to *know yourself*, to *look within*, to *find out who you really are*, because the harder you look, the less you will find, and then you'll realize it was never there in the first place. There isn't a separate you. Your mind is what there is. It's everything. But the only way to find that out is to delve into the state of delusion as hard as possible. Okay, maybe it isn't the *only* way. But it's one way.

Almost all spiritual disciplines—meditations, prayers, and so on—are ways of persisting in folly. They're methods of resolutely and consistently doing what you're already doing. If a person believes the world is flat, you can't talk him out of that. He knows it's flat. He looks out of his window and sees that the world is obviously flat. So the only way to convince him otherwise is to persuade him to go and try to find the edge. Walk due west in a straight manner along the same line of latitude, and you'll eventually get back to the point from where you started. *That* will convince him. And that's the only way to teach him, because people can't be talked out of their illusions.

There is another possibility, but it's more difficult to describe. What if this moment—this one right *now*—is eternity? We have somehow convinced ourselves of the notion that this moment is rather ordinary, that we don't feel very well, that we're vaguely frustrated and worried, and so on, and all this ought to change. But you don't need to do anything at all. *This is it.* And you mustn't try *not* to do anything either, because that's still *doing* something. See—how do you explain that? You can't.

That's why Zen teachers use shock treatment. Zen stories are full of teachers unexpectedly hitting their students or shouting at them or surprising them in some way, because it's that jolt that suddenly brings you *here*. And there's no road to here, because you're already here. It's like the story of the American tourist in England who asks some yokel the way to Upper Tottenham—a little village. The yokel thinks about it, scratches his head, and says, "Well, I do know where it is, but if I were you, I wouldn't start from here."

So whether you ask how you can know God, or how you can attain nirvana, they're the wrong questions. Why do you want nirvana? The fact that you want to attain it is the one thing preventing you from achieving it. You already have nirvana. Of course, it's your privilege to pretend that you don't. If that's your game—to think you're just some ego—well, when you finally want to wake up, you will. Just like that. If you're not awake, it shows you don't want to be awake yet—you're still playing the *hide* part of the game. It's still just the self pretending it's not the self.

When you realize this, the distinction between voluntary and involuntary behavior disappears. The things you think are under your control and the things you think go on outside of you begin to feel exactly the same. You watch other people moving, and you realize it's you making that happen, just as it's you making your blood circulate. At this point, if you don't fully understand, you might go crazy in the sense of feeling you are God in some kind of Jehovah sense of the word—that is to say, that you actually have power over other people and can alter what they're doing. It's not that you discover omnipotence in some crude, literal kind of biblical way. If you actually think that you're Jesus Christ and that everybody ought to fall down and worship you, then you have your wires crossed. You may have had an experience of realization, but you went astray—you didn't know how to interpret it. But if you discover that you are God, you should also see that everybody else is, too.

We open our eyes and look around and think that everything we see is *outside*. It seems that way, because that's how it feels in our head. But there's this space behind the eyes where all this—people sitting around, the colors of the room—is appearing in the nervous system. What we see *out there* is actually a neurological experience. If you realize that—if it hits you as deeply true—then you might assume that all the external world is inside your skull. But you've got your wires crossed. You haven't realized that your skull is in the external world. It's inside you and you're inside it. What kind of situation is this?

The individual and the world don't *interact*—the relationship is *transactional*. For example, when you buy or sell a house, those aspects—buying and selling—can't happen by themselves. There can't be an act of buying unless there's a simultaneous act of selling, and vice versa. In the same way, the relationship between the organism and the environment is transactional—the environment grows the organism, and the organism creates the environment. The organism turns the sun into light, but it requires an environment containing a sun in order to exist. It's all one process. It isn't that organisms came into this world by accident or chance—this world is the sort of environment that *grows* organisms. And it has been that way from the beginning. From the very first moment of the big bang—if that's the way the whole thing started—organisms like you and me were involved.

Here's another example: let's say we have an electric current running through a wire that goes all the way around the earth. Keep in mind that electric current doesn't behave like water in a pipe. At one point we have the positive pole, and at some other place, we have the negative pole, and the current won't even start until the switch is closed from the positive pole. It won't begin unless the point of arrival is there. Now, it might take that current awhile to get going and circuit if it's going all the way around the planet, but the finishing point must be closed before it will even start from the beginning. In the same way, although it took billions of years for primitive life to arise on Earth after the big bang, life was implied from the very beginning. It takes time for an acorn to turn into an oak, but the oak is already implied in the acorn. It's all one process.

Here's what awakening really involves—a reexamination of our common sense. We have all these ideas built into us that seem unquestioned and obvious, and our speech reflects them. "Face the facts" is a common phrase, for example. As if facts were something outside of us, as if life were something we encounter as foreigners. See, our common sense has been rigged. That's why we feel like strangers or aliens in this world, and that separation feels utterly plausible. It's only because that's how we're accustomed to thinking. But when you really start questioning this and exploring other ideas, you see it ain't necessarily so. When you question the basic assumptions that underlie our culture, you find you get a new kind of common sense, and it will become absolutely obvious to you that you are continuous with the universe.

Not too long ago, people believed the earth was flat. They knew it to be true with all their hearts. But then people started sailing all the way around the world and flying from here to there, and we gradually got used to thinking of the earth as globular. We just got used to it. Well, in the same way, it will one day be a matter of common sense to most people that we're all one with the universe. It'll be so simple. And maybe when that happens, we'll handle our technology with better sense. Maybe we'll act with love toward our environment, instead of hate.

PART TWO

THE WEB

OF LIFE

4

Levels of Perception

At the same time that human consciousness is a form of awareness and sensitivity and understanding, it's also a form of ignorance. Our ordinary, everyday consciousness leaves out more than it takes in—things that are terribly important. For example, it leaves out things that would—if we *did* know them—allay our anxieties and fears and horrors. If we could extend our awareness to those things that we leave out, we would experience a deep inner peace, because we would all know the one thing we aren't supposed to know. According to one of the rules of our particular social game, you're simply not allowed to know the lowdown on life. On one hand, *lowdown* means the real dirt on things, but it also means that which is profound, that which is mysterious, that which is in the depths. And the lowdown is that incredibly important aspect of existence that our everyday consciousness screens out.

Our senses are selective. And we are sensitive only to a small band of sensations, so we're missing an enormous range of vibrations outside of that band—cosmic rays, ultraviolet rays, gamma rays, and so on. And I'm also referring to what our instruments are capable of detecting—there are even vibrations that escape their notice. The universe is a vast system of vibrations full of infinite possibilities. When you play a harp, you don't just run your fingers back and forth over all the strings. That makes a terrible sound. You select certain strings in a pattern—you pick out particular notes, and these make a pattern. But at the same time, there are strings you leave out and notes you don't play in the fundamental continuity of the harp.

So what have you left out? That's an absolutely basic question for all of us. You are focused on certain things that constitute what you think of as everyday reality. You single out certain people, certain aspects of buildings, pieces of landscape, parts of the sky, and you actually see the world as a collection of rather disjointed things and events. But you left something out—you forgot something. I'm not talking about your pants or your wig or your glasses, but something absolutely essential. Everyone has forgotten it. And one way to rediscover that thing is through asking the question, "Who are you?"

In response, you might say, "Well, I'm Paul Jones," or whatever your name happens to be. And if I push the issue and say, "No, no, no. Don't give me that stuff. Who are you *really*?" you might take offense or think I'm talking nonsense or playing some kind of trick on you. But really, deep down—who are you? Because that's the thing we've all missed, the thing that's been forgotten, the thing we left out—the underside of the tapestry.

What we are all carefully taught to ignore is that every one of us is an act, a function, a performance, a manifestation of the entire cosmos—what you might call God or Brahman or the Tao. Every one of us is actually *that*, but we are pretending with tremendous skill and deception that we're not. Now, where it's really at is living on two levels at once. If you live the life of your ordinary ego and play your role in life and observe all your particular rules and so on, while at the same time understanding the lowdown, you see the big picture. Then you're what I call a really swinging human being.

But most of us just live on the ordinary level and think that's all there is. So life becomes a drag and we feel we must survive and we work and work at surviving and our children inherit the very same attitude. And nobody has any fun because we're just compulsively trying to get through it all and go on. And people get fed up, you know, and feel like they can't live this way, and some decide to check out and commit suicide. Well, that makes sense in a way. With that attitude toward life, who wants to feel like they *have* to go on living?

Of course, life doesn't have to be that way. Not at all. Life can be quite joyful and spontaneous. The Taoist word for nature means "of itself so"—that is, nature is spontaneous. You don't have to force it; it just happens. I once attended a lecture in New York given by a Zen master I knew. The whole production was quite formal—he was dressed in gold ceremonial robes and sat in front of an altar with candles and a formal little desk for the scriptures. The master was lecturing from a particular sutra to a group of very pious Western devotees. He said, "The fundamental principle in Buddhism is *no purpose*. Purposelessness. When the Buddha needed to fart, he didn't say, 'At nine o'clock, I'm going to drop a fart.' The fart just happens by itself."

So a thing happens of itself. You don't have to tell a fart it *ought* to happen—that puts it in a bind. It's just like telling a child to come and play its game in front of a crowded audience of relatives on Thanksgiving. It absolutely bugs children when you do that. This is the problem for every artist—dancers, musicians, painters, and so on—because artists make their living by playing. And playing on demand, particularly in public at such and such a time, is not an easy thing to learn. My friend Saburo Hasegawa refers to this contrivance as a "controlled accident."

But back to my earlier point: we have been educated to use our minds in a narrow way. We have been taught to ignore that every one of us is an aperture through which the whole cosmos experiences life. Every one of us is a hole from which the fundamental light—existence itself—looks out, but we're playing the game of forgetting this fact, and we pretend to only be this little hole, this little thing we call me, or the ego, or Paul Jones, or whatever. But if we can maintain a sense of being Paul Jones while at the same time understanding we are the whole works, then that's a very marvelous and agreeable arrangement. If you can carry these two perspectives at once, you will experience a most remarkable harmoniousness. It will bring your life a great sense of joy and exuberance, because you know that all the serious predicaments of life are a game.

I'm not saying it's a bad thing to take your individual life seriously. But you could also see your problems and challenges as manifestations of nature, like patterns in waves, or waves in the ocean, or shells upon the beach. Have you really looked at a seashell? There's not an aesthetic fault in it anywhere—it's absolutely perfect. Now, do you think that shells look at each other and critique each other's appearance? "Well, your markings are a little crooked and not very well spaced." Of course not, but that's what we do. Every one of us is marvelous and complicated and interesting and gorgeous just as we are. Really take a look into another person's eyes. They are jewelry beyond compare—just beautiful!

We have specialized in a certain kind of awareness that makes us neglectful of seeing that. We're quite good at briefly concentrated, pinpoint attention. We look at this and we look at that and we select only a handful of certain things from all the things we might possibly be aware of. In doing so, we leave out the experience of amazing beauty in our daily experience as well as the sense of unity with the total process of being. We stare at features in the landscape and ignore the background.

We can also talk about the web of life in terms of magnification. For example, if you examine a piece of embroidery, you'll find it to be an ordered and beautiful object. But if you look at the same object under a microscope, it will appear to be a hopeless tangle of messy threads. But if you zoom in with greater magnification to examine an individual thread, you'll find fantastic order in the most gorgeous designs of molecules. Then if you keep turning up the magnification, you'll find chaos again. Do it again, and you'll see marvelous order. In this way, order and randomness constitute the warp and the woof. We wouldn't know what order was unless we experienced messes.

In the same way, the contrast of on and off, there and not-there, life and death, being and nonbeing, constitutes existence. Only we pretend that the random side of things—this disorderly side of things—could take over and win the competition or, rather, the collaboration. When you lose sight of the fact that the order principle and the chaos principle go together, that's the same predicament as losing sight of the fact that all individually delineated things and beings are connected. Individual mountains stick out of the earth, but there's a fundamental earth underneath all mountains. So all of us are different things that stick out of reality, but there's a continuity underneath, and we ignore that—that's the thing we leave out.

We get hung up on death, but death is merely an interval, an aspect of the wave. Take sound, for example. Everything we call sound is actually *sound/silence*—there's no such thing as pure sound. If there were, you wouldn't be able to hear it. What you actually hear is a series of taps against the eardrum, but it happens so quickly that you get more of an impression of sound than you do of silence. But between every little undulation of sound there is also an interval. When you listen to music and hear the melody, what makes the melody significant are the steps between tones. So the interval *between* whatever happens is just as important as what happens—sound and silence, life and death, warp and woof.

My mother was a great artist in embroidery. She did absolutely fabulous work, and she could do everything with thread—sewing, knitting, tapestries, embroidery. And when I was a child, it always struck me as incredible that string—just thread—could turn into such complex patterned pieces of cloth. Why should it all hang together? My mother took her knitting needles and a ball of wool and improbably turned it all into a sweater. Fantastic! And I found out the secret of it holding together was the combination of warp and woof, the process in which one thread goes under the other, then over the other, then under the other, and so on, until it all just holds up. It's like the example of leaning two sticks together to make them stand up. In the same way, human beings depend on each other—without that mutual support, none of us could exist.

Existence is a function of relationship. Motion is a function of relationship. If you examined a ball in the middle of endless space, you wouldn't be able to tell if it were moving, because there wouldn't be anything for it to move toward or away from. In that situation, motion does not exist. But if we introduce a second ball into the picture, and the two balls were approaching or receding from each other, we could say that one or both were in motion, although we wouldn't be able to decide which was doing what. However, put a third ball into space, and we can assess motion by determining which two balls remain most together, because two is a majority and the universe is basically a democratic organization. Said another way, energy is a form of relationship. The universe is basically a play of energy, and energy and relationship go together.

You know the old riddle: If a tree crashes in a forest and there's nobody there to hear it, does it make a sound? Well, sound requires an eardrum and a nervous system behind the eardrum. We can say that when the tree falls it makes the air vibrate, and if there is anyone around with an ear and an appropriate nervous system, there will be a sound, because sound is a relationship between motion and air and ears. If there's nobody around, the tree falling will make a vibration, but it won't make any sound. In the same way, a star sends light out into space, but the space surrounding the star is dark unless an object—a planet floating by, for example—enters that space. But if there isn't anything in that space to relate to the star, there won't actually be any light there.

One of the most well-known representations of interdependence is the Chinese yin-yang symbol. It looks like two commas curling into one another, or two fish—the white fish has a black eye and the black fish has a white eye. It resembles the shape of a helix, which is the fundamental form of galaxies. It also looks like lovers entwined, or simply two people holding hands. There are two involved, but the two are secretly one.

But in order to see the unitive world that underlies everything, you have to make certain alterations to your common sense. There are ideas and feelings that are difficult to understand—not because they are intellectually complicated, but because they're unfamiliar or estranged. We simply haven't been brought up to accommodate them. Centuries ago, people believed the planets were supported in the sky because they were imbedded in spheres of crystal, and when astrono-mers finally broke the news that there were no crystal spheres, people were confused and felt unbelievably insecure. They had a terrible time assimilating the new version of the cosmos. To understand a com-pletely new idea, you have to do quite a flip. And the new idea that most people have difficulty assimilating is interdependence.

Imagine a spiderweb covered in dew. Every single drop of dew contains within it a reflection of all the other drops of dew. The Japanese use this image to represent the interdependence of everything in the world. Here's a linguistic analogy: *words have meaning only in context*. The meaning of individual words depends upon the sentence or paragraph in which they are found. If I say, "This tree has no bark," that's one thing, and if I say, "This dog has no bark," that's another thing entirely. In exactly the same way, the existence of an individual person is in relation to his or her context. You are what you are sitting here in this very moment in your particular kind of clothes and the particular colors of your face and your particular personality, family involvements, neuroses, everything. You are that precisely in relation to an extremely complex environment. I could even assert that if a given star out in the universe didn't exist, then you would be different from who you are now. I might not say that you *wouldn't* exist, but that you would exist differently. The line of connection between you and the star is very, very complicated, and you might say the connection is faint or unimportant—but it is important. Just because you don't think about it or recognize it doesn't mean it isn't important. You walk on the earth every day without having to ponder how it keeps holding you up, but it does. You might become insensitive and stop thinking about the earth, but it's still there keeping you up.

So, again, existence is relationship. If I put my finger up and nothing touches it—the wind, somebody else—it will stop knowing that it's there. It takes two. And duality is secretly unity. Take the contrast between the very valuable words *explicit* and *implicit*. *Explicit* means what's on the outside—let's say, it's how we appear publicly—and *implicit* means what's going on underneath it all. Politically, look at

Russia and the United States. In public, the two countries make an explicit production of their opposing ideologies—their two differing ways of life—and there has to be a big fight about it all. But behind the scenes, it's all been implicitly worked out and agreed to, because our economy depends on it and their economy depends on it, and everybody knows this who's gotten a little bit wise to the show. A lot of people get taken in by the propaganda, and they should be. Otherwise the whole thing wouldn't work. Tweedledum and Tweedledee have agreed to battle, but underneath opposition there is love, and underneath duality there is unity.

Everything is woven together. As in weaving, things hold together by this over-under, under-over, over-under, and so on pattern that creates fabric, clothing, shelter, matter. The words *matter* and *mater* and *mother* and *maya*—illusion—are related. The world is a marvelous illusion. What is all this made of? What weaves it together? We have tried to understand the world scientifically and explain its mysteries by analyzing the smallest particles we can find, finding smaller and smaller components of matter. And even if we do eventually find a form of basic component that makes all this possible, that infinitely small particle will only be part of the equation. Equally important will be the context in which that particle appears. What does it relate to? Words, sentences, cells, molecules, atoms—everything takes on different properties in different contexts. We've been asking, "What is it?" But we should also explore the questions of *where* and *when*, because that makes all the difference.

A lot of people get anxious with this sort of talk. They don't like to hear that everything is relative. But, really, why get anxious? Relativity isn't some kind of slippery morass in which all standards and rules and directions get lost. Relativity is actually the soundest situation there is.

Explicit and implicit, outside and inside, matter and space, being and nonbeing . . . they're all poles of the same magnet. And if you understand that, you can experience levity and beauty in your relationships with everything. You know, you're not just some tiny *you* hidden in your head, looking out at the world and photographing it with your eyes. If the world weren't there, you wouldn't be here. And vice versa.

We live in a world of animals, vegetables, minerals, atmospheres, and astronomical bodies that's highly intelligent. Its intelligence is concentrated in our brains. The total intelligence of the entire universe crystallizes in human brains—as well as other types of brains—and that's where it *comes out*. But it's still the total intelligence of the entire field. So we go with the whole thing—we interdepend with all of it. We don't just live *in* an environment of rock, air, shrubbery, and so on—that's just a way to explain it when talking about it analytically. We go together with all of these things. We interconnect. Flowers go with bees, humans go with cows, trees go with rain, and so on. Intervals go with sound. But most people are brought up to be tone-deaf in respect to their existence and the rest of the universe. They don't see the unity. They aren't aware of the relationships. But when you spot that, you spot how everything goes together. Then you live a harmonious life.

5

The Web as Trap

So far I've discussed the theme of the web of life from a couple of different perspectives. First, I explained how our attention is selective, which means we constantly create isolates—I'm using that word as a noun—isolates of particular things, events, persons, and so on. This causes us to feel disconnected and alone, because we ignore the connections among and between everything. And that's the first secret we're not taught: supposedly, separate things are actually connected on a fundamental level.

Second, I used the analogy of weaving—threads go underneath and join in back of the embroidery in a way not visible from the front. I don't like using the word *unconscious*, because it makes it sound dead, but let's say that on the unconscious side of life, there are connections that are not published, just as in weaving. In weaving, things intertwine and support each other, and other aspects of existence come into being in the process. And so our world is a manifestation of relativity. This requires a relationship of opposites in every domain of life, and although these opposites are explicitly different and even antagonistic, they are all implicitly one. And that's the second secret: things that seem opposed are inherently mutual and unified.

So let's examine the web in another way. We need different ways of looking at it—we need fullness in our view. So now let's consider the web as a trap—just as a spiderweb is a trap for flies.

Many people already see their lives this way. For some, existence is simply hateful, and they look at the whole of life as a ghastly mistake. Everything lives by eating something else. Kindness and love are merely fronts—pretentions meant to gain advantage over others. From the Darwinian or Freudian point of view, we are all material machines, and our consciousness is simply a very involved and complicated form of chemistry. In this way of looking at things, we might pretend that we aren't heartless, but underneath it all, we are selfish monsters who put on a big act. Basically, all we want to do is eat and screw; we busy ourselves with "higher" things—things we say are the real purpose of life—but really we're just masking our fundamental drives.

And it's partly true. The universe—at least, as far as biology is concerned—is this weird system that lives by everybody eating everybody else. Only we do it in a way that maintains order and civilization. Various species make agreements to not eat each other—they cooperate, form a gang, and go eat other species. And humans are so far the most successful partners in this gangster arrangement. We are the most predatory monsters on earth. We continually assault cows and fish and vegetables and chickens and everything else, only we do it on the sly—most of us never see our food killed. So what we get from the butcher is steak—it has nothing to do with cows. And when we eat fish, it might resemble a fish, but it is no longer the squiggly, squirmy fish that comes from the end of a fisherman's line. See, when you actually catch the fish yourself, you realize that the fish doesn't like it very much. And most of us avoid looking at that extraordinary and terrifying side of things.

The view of the world as a system of mutual exploitation and maximal selfishness is a very profitable view to explore. At some point in your life, you should contemplate two things. First, consider death. Think about skulls and skeletons and imagine going to sleep and never waking up. It's a gloomy thing to think about, but it's like manure in that contemplating death is incredibly generative of creative life. Second, contemplate the notion that you are entirely selfish. Consider that you don't have a good thing to be said about you, and that you are a complete and utter rascal. Now, when you go deeply into the nature of selfishness, what do you discover? What does it mean to love yourself, to seek your own advantage, to be a self that loves itself? It becomes an ever-deepening puzzle.

In what way do I know *me*? I only know me in terms of you. When I think of anything that I know or like, it's always something other than me. Everything I want from a selfish point of view comes from outside of me. There's a reciprocity—a total, mutual interdependence—between what I call me and what I call the other. So if you're perfectly honest about loving yourself and don't pull any punches and don't pretend that you're anything other than exactly what you are, you suddenly come to discover that the self you love is the universe. You don't like all of it—you're still highly selective—but on the whole, you love yourself in terms of what is other. Because it's only in terms of what is other that you have a self at all.

One of Jung's greatest contributions to psychology is the concept of the shadow. Everybody has a shadow. Jung's idea was that the main task of the psychotherapist is to integrate the person with his or her shadow, to put the devil in its proper function. It's always the devil—the shadow, the unacknowledged one, the outcast, the scapegoat, the bastard, the black sheep—who creates. That's where generation comes from. In drama, you need a villain, a certain element of trouble. And in the whole scheme of life, you need the shadow because without it there can't be any substance.

There's an interesting association between crime and all sorts of naughty things and holiness. But holiness doesn't mean being good; good people aren't necessarily holy. A holy person is someone who is *whole*, someone who has reconciled their opposites. And there's always something slightly scary about holy people—other people react to them strangely, as if they can't make up their minds whether or not these people are saints or devils. Throughout history, holy people have always created a great deal of trouble. Take Jesus, for example. The trouble that Jesus created is absolutely incalculable—the Crusades, the Inquisition, and heaven knows what else. Freud, too. They're both incredible troublemakers, but also great healers. It all goes together. Holy people resemble the ocean—on a lovely, sunny day, it appears relaxing and gorgeous, but when a storm comes up, it's absolutely terrifying.

Each of us is an ocean. And Jung felt the whole point was to penetrate our own depths and discover our own motivations with fantastic honesty. But he also knew that nobody can be completely honest—at some point in the exploration of our dark, unconscious depths, there's a certain point when we'll turn away and say, "Well, I've had enough of that." And there's a certain sanity in that—we can't be entirely honest with ourselves. When we look at the web as a trap, deception—particularly self-deception—is paramount.

Humor is an attitude of laughter about oneself. There's a malicious form of humor that laughs at the expense of other people, but the deepest form of humor is about oneself. Why do we laugh at ourselves? Because we know that there's a big difference between what goes on outside and what goes on inside. When you look at a piece of embroidery, the front and back look very different from each other, because people take shortcuts. It's orderly in front and messy in back, and that's how we live. It's like sweeping the dust under the rug right before guests arrive. Our lives are full of ever so many actions like that, and if you don't think that you do it, then you're deceiving yourself. You're just hiding your mess somewhere else, somewhere out of your own awareness. Everybody takes shortcuts, everybody plays tricks, everybody cheats, everybody has within them an element of duplicity and deception. We see it all throughout nature—chameleons changing colors, butterflies that appear to have eyes on their wings, flowers tricking bees. Imagine the consequences if flowers didn't trick bees.

What do you find when you truly explore yourself, when you examine your motivations, when you try to discover that genuine *you* beneath it all? It's like peeling an onion and looking for a pit. It's layer after layer after layer, but where is the center? That's why Zen masters use koans, which require a perfect, genuine, sincere act of searching.

People knock themselves out trying to figure out koans, but the master always catches them, because the master can read their efforts and thoughts. So you have to genuinely explore, but not on purpose. But how then?

When you get stuck thinking that the world is a trap and it sucks you in and you can't escape, go deeper. Don't back away—follow the feeling to its extreme. If you suspect you are selfish, go to the extreme of what selfishness means. Confusion largely results from not following feelings or ideas into their depths. People say they want to live forever, or they want this or that new car, or a certain amount of money to make them happy, and so on, but follow that line of thinking to its end. What would it be like to have those desires fulfilled? When you get caught fantasizing about someone you desire, turn the embroidery around and look at the back. Look at all that mess on the underside, but don't get caught doing it. Do it in secret, because on the front of your embroidery, you're playing the game that everything is just as it's supposed to be. That's what makes you human, and that's what makes you funny.

6

The Web as Play

As I've discussed elsewhere, our senses and consciousness are highly selective. We pick out certain things as significant according to certain game rules, and the game we play most is the survival game. But we mess that game up because the first rule of the survival game is that the game is serious. So watch out. When you play by self-contradictory game rules, the game ceases to be worth the candle, and you start straining and straining, and the game just isn't worth it.

When we listen selectively—when we sense selectively—we miss out on the patterns in the background. The world is basically patterning, and we are patterning organisms. When we eat, for example, we turn food into the patterns of bones, muscles, the nervous system. And sometimes we seek out patterns—we look into microscopes to view the patterns of the small world; we admire the patterns of the cosmos through telescopes; we adorn our homes with the patterns found in paintings; and we admire the patterns of the natural world—the ocean, clouds, birds in flight. Patterns are the universe at play. Even though we don't sing and dance as much as we once did in our culture, our patterning bodies are constantly at play—our hearts, lungs, eyes, capillaries, and so on are all basically dancing.

Can we accept the idea of the web as playful? As not so overly serious? We've been brought up in a cultural context in which the universe is presided over by somebody who is entirely serious. Only in occasional and obscure references in Jewish and Christian scriptures do we find the idea that God dances. The Hindus think otherwise—Shiva and the other gods are commonly represented as dancing. But in our way of looking at things, you must maintain solemn respect, keep entirely silent in church, and heaven forbid you ever laugh. Why not laugh? Is Father Almighty such an insecure fellow that if anyone laughs it will make him uneasy? As if laughter were a challenge to his power? But that's how we've mythologized ultimate reality. God is this cosmic Grand Papa—a stern king who demands, above all things, eternal reverence and respect.

So it's difficult for us to accept the commonsense notion that the web is playful. Imagine the universe as a child who asks, "Won't you come and play with me?" And we have some doubt, some hesitation. We're also a child, and we don't think we should play with the universe. Maybe it comes from the wrong side of the tracks, or maybe we feel we should be doing something else—something serious, like washing dishes for Mother. Incidentally, the whole point of washing dishes is playful. You don't wash dishes for any serious reason—you wash dishes because you want things to look nice. As the Pennsylvania Dutch say, "It's for nice." You like the pattern that way.

But people get terribly compulsive doing things they think they *have* to be doing; they think arranging the patterns of one's life is some kind of duty or debt you owe yourself or others. That's the problem. Parents sometimes play an awful game with their children. Instead of being honest, they say, "We've made such sacrifices for you. We've supported you, paid for your clothes and education, and you've turned out to be an ungrateful little bastard." And the child feels terribly guilty and teaches their children to feel guilty. We've built into our experience the idea that existence is guilt. Some existentialists assert this, you know—the idea that guilt is ontological, that if you're not feeling guilty, then you're not quite human.

You can't make people appreciative by making them feel guilty. That's not the way to make them feel grateful. They might imitate gratefulness and put on a big show and give thanks and acknowledge their indebtedness to you, but it isn't real. And the guilt game from the beginning was an incredible sham. Your father and mother had a great deal of fun bringing you into being—at least, we hope they did—and they wanted to do that in the worst way. So they have no basis for complaint. The guilt game is entirely dishonest.

When people don't admit they're playing games—particularly when they're playing games on you—they're not being fair. That game is rigged. It's played by a person who doesn't really understand that everyday life is a game. It's really important to admit this to ourselves. All truly humane people admit that they're playing a game—that they're rascals, jokers, and tricksters. I've hoaxed you into paying attention to me. It was a trap, you see? But I plan on making it an entertaining trap so that you won't feel so badly about it.

When you go to a concert and listen to somebody play Bach or Mozart or Beethoven, what's the music about? It isn't about anything except the beautiful music—all the various combinations of sounds and melodies going up and down. Existence is like that. It goes one way and then the other, it has hills and valleys, and dark places and light. But that's not the same as saying life is *only* nonsense, or that it's *only* a game.

Have you seen Jan van Eyck's painting of the Last Judgment? It contains everything. In heaven, there's God, the Father; God, the Son; God, the Holy Ghost; the Virgin Mary; and the apostles all in white. The apostles sit in a committee with an aisle between them, just like in church. They're all sitting there very solemnly. At the end of the aisle, you have Saint Michael in beautiful armor and wings, and he's about to bring his sword down on a skeleton with bat wings. And beneath those bat wings lies hell. All horror is let loose there. Nude bodies—some of them quite comely—are being eaten by worms, and there are demons and birds of prey and all sorts of terrible things. And there is no question whatever that van Eyck had more fun painting the lower part of the picture than he did painting the top. Same with those tricksters Hieronymus Bosch and Peter Bruegel the Elder. They loved to paint every detail of every weird, surrealistic devilry going on, even if they couldn't admit that they loved it.

If you are awakened, you learn a particular secret: the web is also a curtain, a veil. It's the veil that hides the face of God from the angels. We're not given the entire picture, you see. It's the same reason we enjoy a good striptease—there's always an implication of something more. You always want a little veil there. It enhances the mystery of it all: What sort of person is this dancer? What would it be like to love her? Does she have bad breath? You never really know. You never get all the way to the bottom of it.

What I'm trying to do is share with you a certain style of life—an attitude to life. I've taken you off to the side and said, "Listen, kids, things aren't what they seem. Don't be fooled. There's a big deception going on, and you're all involved in it." I just think you all ought to know so you can enjoy it. I'm terribly puzzled by people who go out of their way to dis-enjoy themselves. I mean, they take so much trouble to make their lives more miserable! So I don't tell you all these things to say you ought to be awake and this is all a grave matter and you need to arouse your social conscience and so on. No. Because when you do all that, then what? After we've fed the hungry and clothed the naked and made great strides in automation and technology and totally abolished polity, then what are we going to do?

To spread joy, you need to have joy. To impart delight, you have to be—more or less—delightful. You don't do this by *appearing* delightful, but by doing things and living a life that is delightful to you. People who are interesting are people who are *interested*. A person who thinks about all sorts of things and is fascinated by people and life becomes a fascinating person. But a person who doesn't think about anybody else is boring. In other words, the more you are engaged with the external world, the more you are enriched. But if you try to enrich your personality by taking a course on how to win friends and influence people, or how to be a "real" person, or how to be a spiritual person, or what-have-you, it doesn't work. It doesn't work that way.

If I just yell a monotone yell with no rhythm to it at all, it won't be long until you tell me to cut it out. It's annoying—nobody wants to hear that. Or you'll stop hearing that sound eventually, because your consciousness will become insensitive to it. What we long to hear is the gap, the break. Those silences create the rhythm, and more complex patterns of silences create even more interesting rhythms. That's where we can be surprised. But dull people don't do that. They put their hats on straight, eat the same thing every day, go to the same office, and so on. It's the same song—day in, day out.

But if you truly explore yourself and go deeper and deeper into your own nature, you'll find that you're a rhythm. What's more, you'll discover you're a rhythm doing a rhythm, and beneath that another rhythm doing a different rhythm. Everything vibrates. Everything is rhythm. But who's the musician? Who's setting the beat? They disappeared. We looked for them, and they just vanished, then they came around again when we weren't looking. But every time we try to see them, they aren't there. And that's the situation of this thing called life.

PART THREE

INEVITABLE

ECSTASY

7

Attachment and Control

When we were babies, we didn't know anything other than what we felt, and we didn't have names for that. As we grew older, we learned to differentiate one thing from another, one event from another, and ourselves from everything else. And that's all well and good as long as we don't forget the foundation. Mountains are differentiated from one another, but their foundation is the same, and we might have different words for different mountains, but there aren't any words for their foundation, because words are only for distinctions. And there can't really be a word—or an idea, for that matter—for nondistinction. We can feel it, of course, but we can't *think* it. We feel that we're conscious, but we don't know what consciousness itself is, because consciousness is present in every conceivable kind of experience. Presumably, a fish doesn't know anything about water, because it never leaves water.

However, when we grow up, we forget the foundation. We become fascinated, spellbound, and enchanted by all the things adults wave at us, and we forget the background. We come to think that all these distinctions we've learned about are the most important things to be concerned with, and we become hypnotized. We get stuck focusing on flashy distinctions that we think truly matter. In Buddhism, that sense of mistaken stuckness is called *attachment*.

Attachment doesn't refer to things like enjoying dinner or appreciating beauty or sleep, and it isn't about certain responses like fear or sorrow.

These are all natural responses of our organism to its environment. The Sanskrit word is *klesha*, and a better translation than "attachment" might be the slang term "hang-up." You know, we get hung up on this or that thing—we get stuck or blocked or can't remove ourselves from a state of waggly hesitation. That's what's meant by the term *klesha*. We get these hang-ups about all types of things, and we are taught to have hang-ups by our parents and aunts and uncles and teachers and peer group. And two major hang-ups we're taught from early childhood are the distinction between ourselves and others and the distinction between voluntary and involuntary actions. This is immensely confusing to a small child. For example, it's told to go to sleep or have a bowel movement or love its parents or stop being anxious, but all these things are just supposed to happen on their own. So the child is commanded to do what will please its elders and betters, but it must be done spontaneously. It's no wonder that we're all so confused.

In response, we develop this thing called *ego*. Now, I want to be clear what I mean by ego. I don't mean something synonymous with our particular living organism, but something rather abstract. The ego has the same function and kind of reality as an hour or an inch or a pound or a line of longitude. It's for purposes of discussion, for convenience. We have an ego due to social convention, but the fallacy we all make is that we treat this abstraction as if it were something real and physical. But the ego is merely a composition of ideas and images about ourselves. This image is obviously no more *us* than the idea of a tree is *tree*.

Additionally, the image we carry about ourselves is extremely inaccurate and incomplete. My image of me is not at all your image of me, and my image of you is not at all your image of you. Furthermore, my image of me leaves out all manner of information regarding my nervous system, circulation, metabolism, and all sorts of subtle relationships with the surrounding human and nonhuman universe. In other words, the image I have of myself—my ego—is a caricature. I arrived at this image mainly through my interaction with other people who told me who I was in one way or the other—either directly or indirectly—and I play that picture of myself out into the world, and the world plays it back.

And from early on, we're told that this picture—this image—must be consistent. For a lot of people, the quest for identity means searching for an acceptable image. *What role am I supposed to play? What am I supposed to do in life?* Those questions are important, but they are extraordinarily misleading unless they're backed up by deeper matters.

You might protest and say that you don't think of yourself as just an image. You might say that you feel more real than that, that you are the center of something. Well, let's take a look. Who are you in terms of your body? If you look at yourself, all you can see are your feet and legs and belly and arms and hands and some vague part of your nose if you close one eye. And you assume you have a head because everyone else has a head. Or you looked in the mirror, and the mirror reflected your head back to you. But you never really see your head, just as you never really see your back. So, naturally, you put your ego in that unseen part of your body, because that seems to be where it all comes from, and you can *feel* it. But what is it that you feel? If I see clearly—if my eyes are in functioning order—my eyes aren't conscious of themselves. I mean, unless I see spots or detect some kind of deficiency in vision, I don't notice that I'm seeing. So if my ego is working properly, why should I be aware of it as something sort of *there*? That's just a nuisance—something in the way—especially since the ego is awfully difficult to take care of. So that can't be what we *feel*.

What we feel is a kind of chronic, habitual sense of muscular strain. And that's what we learned as children when we were taught to perform spontaneous activities on command. We feel that tension when someone tells us to "look carefully" or "pay attention." We try to use our muscles to make our nerves work, which is futile and actually gets in the way of the nerves working properly. We hold our breath, we control our emotions, we tighten our stomachs and rectums out of fear, we "pull ourselves together." This chronic tension in Sanskrit is called *sankocha*—contraction—the root of what we call the feeling of ego. This feeling of tightness is the physical referent for the psychological image of ourselves.

The ego is naturally useful for social communication—I'm this idea of a being with a particular name. That works fine provided we know what we're doing and take it for what it is. But we're so hung up on this concept that it confuses us even in the proposition that it might be possible for us to feel otherwise. When we hear about people transcending the ego, we think, "Gosh, how did they do that?" That's a ridiculous thing to think. They "transcended" the ego because it was never really there in the first place. You can't transcend the ego any more than you can cut a wheel of cheese with a line of longitude.

Let's suppose you're a baby again. You don't know anything. All these words are just noise. Don't try to make it otherwise—don't make any effort. Naturally, you'll feel certain tensions in your body, or words or ideas will drift through your mind, but it's just like the wind blowing, or clouds moving across the sky. Don't bother with any of that—you don't have to get rid of anything. Just be aware of what's going on in your body and mind just as you might be aware of clouds in the sky. There's no problem with any of it. Just look and feel and listen without naming, and if you *are* naming, that's okay—just watch that. You can't force anything here. You can't willfully stop thinking or stop naming. Do you notice? This doesn't mean you're bad at meditating—it's not a sign of defeat. It's just illustrating that everything runs on, all by itself. It's just showing you that an individual, separate you is a figment of your imagination. So remember: you're a baby. You feel things happening, but you don't know anything about the difference between those things and you. No one has taught you that distinction yet. Nobody has taught you that what you see out in front of you is either near or far from your eyes. Let's call everything you sense and feel *this*. It's everything that's going on. It's what the Chinese call Tao, or what the Buddhists call *suchness* or *tathata*. And it's not happening to *you*, because what is *you*? You're just an aspect of the happening.

So who's in control around here? That's a strange notion—that there's someone or something in control. As if processes require something outside of themselves to control themselves. Why can't processes be self-controlling? We say, "Control yourself!" as if you could split a person in two, with one part separate from the self that's supposed to be controlled. How can that achieve anything? How can a noun start a verb? Yet it's a fundamental superstition we have that this can be done. You have this spontaneous process going on that's controlling itself, aware of itself—aware of itself through you. You are an aperture through which the universe looks at itself. And because it's looking at itself through you, there's always an aspect of itself that it can't see. And this results in a game of hide-and-seek. But when you ask, "Who is doing the seeking?" you are still working under the assumption that every verb needs a subject. If you assert that knowing requires a knower, you're simply applying particular grammatical rules to nature. However, many languages use verbs without nouns, and when you actually look for doers as distinct from deeds, you can't find them, just as you can't find any "stuff" underlying the patterns of nature. What we call stuff is simply patterns seen out of focus.

We use these words—energy, matter, being, reality, Tao, universe. Did you know that *universe* means "one turn"? It's your turn now. You turn to look at yourself. But you can't make two turns to see what's looking! As they say in Zen, you can't grasp it and you can't get rid of it, and in not being able to grab it, you get it.

This is what gurus have used to trick you into seeing. All these trials they put you through are simply to convince you that you can't do anything about it, but not "convince you" in a theoretical way. I'm not a guru—I don't give individual spiritual direction to people—so maybe it's not the best thing that I'm giving away the guru's tricks, but I might as well. You can struggle and struggle and struggle, and you will do so for as long as you have the feeling inside you that you're missing something. And everyone will encourage you to think this way, because they also feel they're missing something, and they think they can get it by such and such a method, so they're going to try to convince you that their method is the thing to do.

Gurus use this behavior to beguile their students. The guru gives tasks that might seem difficult, but can be accomplished—this gives you a feeling of making progress. But the guru also assigns tasks that are impossible, and these are what you'll get hung up on. And the possible exercises will make you double your efforts in solving the impossible ones. There might be multiple ranks or levels through which you can advance, just like degrees in masonry or belt levels in judo. Different stages of con-sciousness—that sort of thing. And because you retain this sense of something missing, you get in competition with yourself and others, but all this effort and competition and searching is just like looking for your own head. You can't see it, so you might imagine you've lost it. And that's the point. We don't see what looks, so we think we've lost it. So we go off in search of ourselves or God or the atman or whatever, but it's the one thing we can't find—because we're already it.

So you can't do anything to find it. And if you tell yourself, "Well, then there's nothing I can do about it," why did you say that? Why might you go out of your way to note that futility? It's because there's a funny feeling you have that if you tell yourself that there's nothing you can do about it, something different will happen. But even that doesn't work. Nothing works. And when absolutely nothing works, where are you? The world doesn't stop—things keep happening. That's what I'm talking about—there's this *happening* going on when you aren't doing anything about it; there's this *happening* going on when you aren't *not* doing anything about it. That's the point. It goes on despite anything you think or worry about.

You might call this determinism, but you'd be wrong. There is no one being determined. And if you conceive of determinism as the direction of what happens by the past—the idea that the past causes the present and future—you're hallucinating. The present does not come from the past. You can realize this yourself by closing your eyes and listening to the sounds around you. Where do they come from? You hear them coming out of silence—they come and go like echoes in the labyrinth of your brain. Sounds don't come from the past—they come from the present and trail off. You can do this exercise with your eyes, too. For example, you're watching someone on television—look at their hands. When they move, we think that the movement is caused by the hands and that the hands were there before, and so they can therefore move after. We don't see that our memory of the hands is an echo of there always being *now*. They never *were*, they never *will be*—they're always *now*. The motion of the hands is recollected like the wake of a ship—the wake doesn't move the ship. And the past doesn't move the present, unless you insist that it does.

Eventually, you will become aware that this happening isn't happening *to* you, because you are the happening. The only you there is *is* what's going on. Feel that and disregard the stupid distinctions you've been taught, because they won't help you to feel the happening genuinely. And understand that all of this isn't determined. You will experience an odd feeling of synthesis between doing and happening—doing is as much a happening as happening is, and happening is as much a doing as doing is. This is the profound experience some people have that—outside of the proper understanding—can lead them to proclaim themselves as the omnipotent God Almighty in the Hebrew or Christian sense. Well, you are omnipotent, but not in that way. I am omnipotent insofar as I am the universe, but I am not omnipotent in the role of Alan Watts, only cunning.

With this in mind, let's examine the question of pain and our so-called reactions to it. Once again, you will see that when you look at the problem this way, it immediately sets up a duality of pain on one side and the person who suffers it on the other. It should be evident, then, that a great deal of the energy of pain is derived from the resistance offered to it. That resistance can take many forms. You might try to run away from a migraine, for example, and quickly realize that you can't—that it seems to be absolutely in the middle of everything, and however much you resist it, the pain follows you. A lot of this type of pain is doubly problematic because of our prior anxiety about it as well as all the judgments we have about pain. For example, in a hospital, it is taboo to scream, because the hospital is not run for you—it's run for the convenience of the staff. Everything is done in a way so as to interiorize localized pain. So we have a big social problem, right from the beginning, about our reaction to anything painful. For example, when a child eats something that doesn't agree with her, and she vomits, everyone says, "Ugh!" But the experience of vomiting is actually one of release—it's a pleasant release from the suffering of an upset stomach. So people learn from their parents or teachers that vomiting is nasty, just as they learn that excrement is nasty, just as they learn that anything associated with death and disease is unpleasant. But there really isn't anything radically wrong with being sick or with dying.

Who said you were supposed to survive? Who gave you the idea that it's preferable to go on and on and on? Obviously, we can't go on living—we'd overcrowd ourselves, for one thing. So, in actuality, a person who dies is honorable, because he or she is making room for others on the planet. Nothing else is workable. Even if we could live forever and ever, we'd eventually realize that it wasn't the way we wanted to survive. Why else have children? Children are our survival. We pass the torch on to them—you don't carry the torch forever; you offer it to someone else. It's a far more amusing arrangement for nature to continue the process of life through different individuals than by doing it through the same individuals forever.

When we look at life in terms of survival and profit, we miss out on the magic. Watch children—everyday things are marvelous to them because they see these things in a fresh manner not related to survival or profit. Even scratches on the floor possess magic for a child. And since over time we cease to see the magic in the world, we no longer fulfill nature's game of being aware of itself, so we die. There's no point to life otherwise. Someone new comes along, appreciates the world with entirely fresh eyes, and nature's self-awareness game continues on as a game worth the candle.

It's not natural for us to want to prolong life indefinitely. However, we live in a culture that tries to convince us at every turn that death is a terrible thing, that death must be swept under the carpet. For example, look at how we treat the elderly in hospitals. Grandma is dying, she suspects that she is dying, but the family and doctor conspire to keep from Grandma the very obvious fact that she is dying. For some reason, the family has this funny feeling that it's important to build up courage and hope, so they lie: "Oh, you're getting better—you'll probably be up and about in a couple of weeks." A mutual distrust develops, because once you're playing the game on that level, you tend to play the mistrust out on other levels. And Grandma is left to die alone—suddenly, unprepared, and doped up to the point where death occurs without any spiritual experience of it whatsoever.

When I was in Zurich in 1958, I met a most extraordinary man by the name of Karlfried von Dürckheim. He was a former Nazi agent who had been sent to Japan to disseminate propaganda. He wound up studying Zen and experienced a spiritual rebirth while being imprisoned after the war, eventually returning to Germany and opening a meditation center in the Black Forest. He devoted his work to people who had undergone spiritual crises during the war, and what he found, time and again, was people who had experienced what he termed "natural satori" under the threat of death. People had heard the bombs coming—they had heard that particular whistle—and they had known they were headed right for them. Well, what happened was that these people—who knew they were finished—had accepted it. And when they accepted it, they had a strange feeling that everything was absolutely clear, that everything in the entire universe was just as it should be—every grain of dust in the universe was in exactly the right place. And they completely understood at that moment what everything was all about, only they couldn't describe it. So these people with these profound experiences would try to talk to their families about what they had seen and felt, but no one would listen: "Oh, you were under a lot of pressure—you were probably hallucinating." That sort of thing. But Dürckheim listened to them and believed that these weren't hallucinations, but exceedingly rare examples of people actually waking up.

This is the opportunity presented by death. If you can go into death with eyes open and the support of others, this extraordinary thing can happen to you. And from that vantage point, you'd say, "I wouldn't have missed that opportunity for the world! Now I understand why we die!" The reason we die is to give us the opportunity to understand what life is all about, and we can only experience that when we let go, because it is only then that we come to a situation that the ego can't deal with. When we are no longer hypnotized, our natural consciousness can see clearly what all this universe is for. But we miss this opportunity. We institutionalize death out of the way instead of encouraging a social acceptance of death, instead of rejoicing in death. I'm not saying that at our deathbed we need laughter and balloons and presents; I'm just saying we need a new approach. Instead of putting on long faces and making a sad show out of it—particularly Christians, who presumably believe they're going to heaven—we owe it to ourselves to work out an entirely new approach to death.

It's understandable that some people die with concerns about their spouse and children. However, no one is indispensable, and there comes a point when you have to say, "I'm sorry, but I am going to abandon all of my responsibilities, because there's nothing else I can do." That's another form of surrender. When you drop everything in this way, a curious thing happens—it dawns on you that to be important, existence does not have to go on. It needn't last any more than a moment. Quantitative continuity has little value. How long can you hold your breath? Who cares!

We don't have to suffer being bombed or put into concentration camps. In this very moment, we can be as those about to die. We can genuinely and honestly understand the mystery of life, because death is—in a certain sense—the source of life. In the forest, leaves die and fall off the tree to the forest floor. They mold and rot and supply humus from which more plants grow. That's the cycle.

But we try to stop that cycle from happening. Look at what morticians do—make the body unpalatable to worms, as if being eaten were an indignity to the human being. Why? We eat everything else, and we give nothing back. That's a symptom of our profound disorientation with respect to death. Not only do we consider death an indignity, but we also send pregnant women to hospitals for the most unnatural, weird kind of birthing. More and more, we regard the healthy and inevitable and natural transformations of the body as pathological.

Soon we'll have to have sexual intercourse on operating tables to make sure the whole operation is hygienic! More and more, everything about us is becoming interfered with by specialists, while less and less we consider our lives the province of our own preferences. We can't even die in our own way without going to the hospital and being fed through tubes and wasting the family's savings. For what? It's even a crime to commit suicide. This is simply nonsense.

But let's get practical. You might argue that this is all fine and good, but once you are told you're going to die, you will undoubtedly look for a way out of it and go into some sort of panic. And this panic in the face of death is in you in some uncontrollable way—you have an instinct to survive, and the instinct arises as this panic. Okay, let's take another step. You might also feel ashamed of that panic, even though you've been taught to do everything possible to survive. You might feel as if you're supposed to face death calmly and bravely and *not* be panicked. Well, if you are in a panic and can't stop, that's another opportunity. Just as people experience profound insight at the moment of death because they can't do anything whatsoever to prevent it, so too can panic provide the same opportunity for enlightenment. However, if you think, "I *must* stop panicking," then all that will happen is greater confusion and panic—you'll be at cross-purposes with yourself.

Old-fashioned preachers went on and on about death. Catholic monks kept human skulls on their desks. In baroque times, they made tombstones covered with marvelous sculptures of skeletons and bones. Some churches in Rome contain crypts with altar furnishings made entirely from the bones of departed monks. Tibetan Buddhists practice graveyard meditation, even using trumpets made from human thighbones and ritual cups made from human skulls, richly worked in silver and turquoise. From our point of view today, all this is very morbid. But what's the problem? What's blocking us from contemplating death regularly like this? You might say it's because it scares you, that death gives you the heebie-jeebies. Okay, then. So death isn't the problem—the heebie-jeebies are the problem.

So let's deal with the heebie-jeebies in a familiar way—don't try to stop them or ignore them, because they're very valuable. They won't stop you from dying, but you can learn from them the same thing you can learn from dying.

But the social pressure to resist fear is terrific. Heebie-jeebies and fears are just not permissible. What's the reasoning behind this? I think we have this cultural assumption that if you're afraid, you can't perform under pressure. Basically, we think that if you have the heebie-jeebies, you can't be a good soldier—you'll just crumble under the weight of your fear. This is nonsense. Courageous people are often those who are quite frightened—courageous action isn't a consequence of having no fear.

Additionally, I think we also suppress the heebie-jeebies because of their orgiastic aspects. Extreme situations—terror, extreme pain, and so on—involve the same sort of physiological oscillating process as sexual orgasm, and we get embarrassed by that because it conflicts with our image of ourselves as composed and in control. If you looked at a photo of your face during sexual rapture but didn't understand the context, you wouldn't be able to tell if you were in pleasure or pain. A tide of vibrations has taken over your whole being, as if you were in the possession of a god, and that's taboo.

Some of you might think this discussion is getting out of line because we're moving into an uncomfortable or "perverse" topic, but here we go. The two primary forms of what we call perverse experiences are sadism and masochism, both of which associate pain with ecstasy. Even if we think this sort of thing is pathological, it's actually quite common, and I'm referring here to a situation where sadists and masochists happily meet, when the combination of the two is voluntary and perfect. There's an important principle at work here. Pain and the attendant convulsive behavior of the organism are associated with the erotic—a different value is given to the symptoms. In the total abandonment to those sensations, it's possible to feel united with what's happening—completely at one. That's what we all aspire to. The masochist is someone who has learned to defend against pain by eroticizing it, but it's simply a matter of placing different valuations on the same vibration.

All we experience is a spectrum of vibrations—light, sound, smell, tactile feelings, emotions, everything. We live in the midst of a woven tapestry in which the warps and woofs are all these different spectra of various kinds of vibrations. If you didn't have one, you wouldn't have the other, because it takes two to reveal the pattern. We are patterns in a weaving system. We wouldn't be here if it weren't for the interlocking of all these different spectra of dimensions. And when a vibration reaches a certain point, we think it's too much, and when it falls to a different point, we think it's not enough. At one end, it's so subtle that we might go to sleep, but at the other end, it might feel as if things were going to rip right apart, and someone in that experience of tension might panic, and we'll tell that person to relax and take it easy. But you can't often do that. So for the person who can't relax, I say go into that tension. Go in the direction of least resistance—scream, get violent inside, that sort of thing. One way or the other, it doesn't matter which way you go when the boat of life begins to rock, but I think you might as well rock with it than against it.

Ecstasy is inevitable. It doesn't matter which road we take to get there. In a way, ecstasy is the nature of existence—a universe exists for the simple reason that it is ecstatic. What else are these fireworks about? When you know that everything is all right and that the situation is inevitable ecstasy, you won't make such a fuss about everything. And the question, "What shall I do?" disappears, as it should have in the beginning, because there was never a real *I* there in the first place. The question will bring you back to the experience itself. Some people hear this and immediately worry that this understanding will lead to everyone becoming totally callous and impassive, and I can't assure you that this won't happen. But if you experience this state of being, you'll find out for yourself.

8

Hypnosis and Habituation

We commonly think that children—particularly, babies—are inferior in view to adults. If an adult showed signs of a baby's undifferentiated, nonselective awareness, psychologists would call this "regression." In actuality, we need the baby's view as the basis for the adult view because, if we don't have that basis, we take the adult view—selective awareness—far too seriously. We get completely carried away. It's like someone playing poker and losing their nerve because they have forgotten that it's only a game, so he or she becomes a very bad player. In life, we're all playing a game, but we've forgotten that, because we've lost the infant's way of seeing. But what we actually need is both ways of seeing—that's a Buddha's view. We know both, so we aren't taken in by adult games, although we're perfectly capable of playing them. It's just that we don't take them too seriously.

When we ask how we can recapture the baby's point of view, that's the wrong question, because it arises entirely and exclusively out of the adult's point of view. The adult way of viewing things thinks there is an *I* that exists independent of everything else, but this sense of an isolated *I* is merely a convention—it has no fundamental reality. And so long as we don't understand that, we're confused. The only way to regain a child's view is to realize that you can't do anything about it at all—you can't even do *nothing* about it. All possibilities of vision for what I call *I* are out. So long as you are trying or not trying, you are aggravating the sensation of a separate ego. That presents a certain difficulty, or so it seems.

And it's not just the ego that's an illusion, but the whole valuation system we place on everything. All these distinctions we make about the complexity of vibrations we call life—all the valuations manufactured by the social game—are maya. It's only play when we say one thing is good and another is bad, or one event is advantageous and another is disadvantageous. You might think this hypnosis is impossible to overcome—that not thinking that way is unthinkable. Of course, you have to think that. The process of hypnosis has put into you the suggestion that you forget the whole thing, that all these learned rules are sacrosanct. We've been hypnotized this way ever since we were receptive children.

It's part of the conspiracy we play on ourselves. We can't blame our parents, because their parents played the same con on them. We can't blame this on the past. We're creating the values of the past right now in the present—we're buying them all along. Psychology has ensured that American parents are consumed with guilt about the way they bring up their children, but we must abandon completely the notion of blaming the past for any kind of situation we're in. We must reverse our thinking and see that the past always flows back *from* the present—*now* is the creative point of life. For example, when you forgive someone, you change the meaning of the past. Or when you're reading a sentence in German or Latin where the verb awaits you at the very end, it's only then that you find out what the sentence means. The present is always changing the past.

So when you tell yourself that you can't obtain this undifferentiated, open way of seeing, don't take that thought too seriously. It's simply a method of postponing realization. You can keep putting it off—that's perfectly okay. There's no real reason or compulsion for why you should come out of this illusion. Notice that Buddhists don't tend to be missionaries in the same way as Western people. It isn't urgent that you be "saved" unless you think so. Unless you are so disturbed by the problem of suffering and you just need to find an escape. Otherwise, no hurry—there's lots of time. Maybe you'll see through it all when you die—at the moment of death you'll see that it was all a fake. So don't be put off or frightened by the difficulty of seeing through the illusion. That's a red herring, and it's quite irrelevant.

Teachers will tell you that your realization is going to take a long, long time and only after a lot of practice. Maybe it will, maybe it won't. Really, it's beside the point—it's distracting. If I recommend a book to you and tell you that it is incredibly difficult to read and will require years of your life and immense powers of concentration, well, that will likely just kill your interest in the book. I should say something like, "This is a most extraordinary book. It's just fascinating. I've been reading it for years, and every time I pick it up, I get so involved that I just can't put it down!" Isn't that a more encouraging attitude?

If we can see that the ego is purely fictitious—that it is merely an image of ourselves coupled with a sensation of muscular strain occasioned by trying to make this image an effective agent to control emotion and direct the nervous operations of our organism—then it becomes clear that what we have called *ourselves* isn't able to do anything at all. If we realize that, a kind of silence follows in which there is nothing to do except watch what happens. But what is happening is watching itself. There is nobody apart from it watching it.

And what about the other illusions? Although they are integrated with the illusion of ego, the whole value system—what's important, good, bad, pleasant, painful, and so on—can be called into question. Not in order to destroy the system, but in order to see it for what it is. Again, you might object and think that seeing through these valuations is a colossally difficult task, because you've been habituated to it your whole life, and you think the longer you have been habituated to something, the more difficult it is to change it. That's only true if you believe it. It's not true if you don't believe it.

Zen emphasizes immediate action. When anything is to be done, it should be done immediately without thinking it over in advance. You'll find this to be a characteristic of people who have been trained in Zen—they don't sit around and debate with themselves about how to do something, they just do it. So you don't have to hem and haw about calling into question your whole value system—just do it. You might be in the habit of eating a roast beef sandwich for lunch every day, but at any moment, you can choose to try a smoked salmon one, and you don't have to put a lot of thought into it. Just eat a different sandwich.

We have been conditioned to assess this complex of vibrations as good, bad, pleasant, painful, and so on. But, as a matter of fact, they're nothing but vibrations. And if you try to look at any one of them by itself, you won't be able to find it. That is to say, if you only know red, you don't know that it's red—you only know it's red in contrast to yellow and green and blue and violet. You don't know that a particular sound is loud unless you are familiar with soft sounds. These comparisons give us the feeling of the spectrum as being varied—otherwise we wouldn't know. So we can see that all the values we place on these vibrations are arbitrary—they're just vibrations. And if you think this is all nonsense, you're correct. This is how the universe works. A lot of music is nonsense—it doesn't mean anything, but it can be very interesting. When you were a child, you often took delight in perfectly meaningless things—for example, those door stoppers with springs that make a *boing* sound. *Boing, boing, boing*—that's fascinating! It doesn't mean anything—it's just *boing*. And if you really get into that *boing* sound, you can see the whole universe in *boing*, because each vibration implies all others.

Vibrations are fascinating. We have a tendency to take such an interest in vibrations that we're willing to risk danger to do so. Children are always daring each other to do something forbidden, because the risk of calamity or disapproval makes the game so exciting. For the same reason, adults challenge disaster with all manner of wildly adventurous activities—skydiving, for example—because that provides a certain vibration they find extremely interesting. Why the craving for speed, and so on? You can only get this if you look at a vibration very closely—for example, repeating a mantra or phrase or your own name over and over and over and over again. After a while it becomes meaningless—it's just noise. But the sound isn't just noise. That's just an adult attitude about the experience. A child doesn't hear *boing* and think, "Well, that's just a noise." A child understands that sound is just fantastic.

The whole world is energy at play—it's a kaleidoscope of jazz. You can really get into that and pay attention to a certain vibration and realize that is the whole point of being alive. But other people won't like it. The guardians of the game will accuse you of doing something very dangerous, or they'll call you crazy. Theological texts are full of fear that the universe is meaningless, and that fear pervades our culture, but only because people haven't dared to look. And people with severe depression perceive the world as meaningless, but worse—a conspiracy of horror, for example. Well, if you imagine that everything is mechanical—that we're basically fleshy computers in some grand clockwork system—you get a sense of the world as plastic, tasteless, or hollow. But that's still a valuation. If you think this is the way of the world, you're devaluing the mechanical and praising the organic, just as we don't enjoy a plastic flower because it doesn't have a scent. But the world is neither organic nor mechanical, and it is neither voluntary nor involuntary—it is simply what it is, beyond the categories of our contrasting, selective awareness. Seeing through that, we experience what the Buddhists call suchness or tathata, based on the word *that*. That, that, that. That's what's going on.

In some meditative states, you can see everything as *that*. And you don't immediately evaluate that as meaningless, because if you see the world as an illusion, you can still choose to take the world quite seriously, but you'll always know in the back of your mind that it's a game. So you can get involved in life to a ridiculous degree, because you know it's all right—it's just vibrations. That's why enlightened people—even *bodhisattvas*—aren't detached and indifferent. They're perfectly free to enjoy and suffer emotions and attachments. R.H. Blyth, who was a great Zen man, once wrote me, "How are you these days? As for me, I have abandoned satori altogether and I'm trying to become as deeply attached as I can to as many people and things as possible." So you might normally approach life cautiously, but seeing the world as *that* makes it possible for you to become much more involved—to feel, love, and throw yourself at the mercy of these goings-on completely. The very perception of the illusion makes it possible to live up to the illusion.

If you see someone who carries a detached and reserved attitude toward life, it just indicates they are fearful of getting involved. I can't understand that very well. What do people expect? That an enlightened person shouldn't need this, that, and the other? That they can't appreciate beauty or sexual attraction? It seems some spiritual people want to scrub everything down, like they want to scrub the planet clean of this disease called life, and enjoy a nice, clean rock. Well, I believe in color. If we're going to participate in this illusory dance, then let's really live it up. Let's not take ourselves so damn seriously! We don't need to be scrubbed of ornamentation and frivolity.

It all depends on being able to get back to that point in meditation. But don't misunderstand that. I don't mean to enter a state of expectation day after day to improve your awareness—meditation doesn't work like that. So just do it. Eventually, as time goes on, you will really see the world. In meditative consciousness, you will see that nothing is more important than anything else. And there is no such thing as wasting time, because what is time for except to be wasted? Just sit and do nothing. Meditation is the perfect waste of time.

9

Harmonious Dissolution

Let's get down to the nitty-gritty. The universe is a transitory system—like a bubble, or smoke, or foam on water. It comes and goes and dissolves, but we don't want that. We don't want to give up and go along with the dissolution, but what do we think we're going to get by holding on and resisting? I'm not preaching at you to give up. I just want you to get in touch with what it feels like inside when you contemplate the prospect of nothing—that this whole thing is just a bubble that dissolves. Mostly, when people think about death, they get cold, lonely, or scared, because death is an unknown. And the most frightening thing about death is that there might be something beyond it, and we don't know what that is.

For children and some adults, the world seems full of danger. There are monsters everywhere, and behind every monster is death—dissolution is the end of it all. By and large, governments fill that feared void beyond death with threats of a rather unspecified nature in order to maintain control. As long as we're scared of those threats and think that death is a bad thing, we can be ruled. This is why no government likes mystics. Mystics understand that you have to have nothing to have something. Mystics don't fear death, so you can't scare them.

What is it that we fear? What do you imagine it's like to go to sleep and never wake up? It can't be like a state of being buried alive or being in the dark forever, because that would require an experience of darkness.

I had the most interesting discussion recently with a young woman who was born blind. She doesn't know what darkness is—the word is absolutely meaningless to her, because she's never seen light. Do you see darkness behind your eyes? Behind the visual field, you can't see darkness or light—there is simply nothing conceivable at all. So consider that area of blankness we call death to be what lies behind the eyes. That's what we can't think about.

Here's something else to imagine: your life—your sense of vitality, importance, aliveness of being—is simply a sudden experience. It was nothing before it started, and it will be nothing after it's over. That's the simplest possible thing you could believe in—it requires no intellectual effort, really. Now, what's your feeling about that? Let's suppose you feel sorrow. For whom is this sorrow? When it's all over, who will there be to feel sorry? When it's all come to an end, nobody will be there to feel sorrow or regret or happiness—that will be that. Well, let's look at it from the other direction: suppose all this would *never* come to an end. So you're stuck there feeling sorrow and regret and happiness and misery over and over again, and the whole thing never stops—that's a depressing thought, isn't it? So how about a compromise? Imagine that the whole thing disappears all together, but then it starts over again, and when it starts over again, it will feel precisely as it does now—that all this never happened before.

In Hindu thought, the universe lasts for 4,320,000 years and then it vanishes. Then it restarts and runs for another 4,320,000 years, and it vanishes. Then it does it again. And again and again and again, and there's no end to that cycle, but our forgetting about it means it doesn't become a total insufferable ball. Between every crest of a wave, there's a trough. The Hindus saw that and contemplated the thought of *moksha*—liberation from the everlasting cycle of appearing and disappearing. And then the Buddha came along and taught his particular way out of *samsara*—the wheel of birth and death—and others came along and said, "Well, isn't that rather selfish? You get out, but what about everyone else?" Which is why the Buddha taught how to come back again and help everybody else in a very sophisticated way: Nirvana and samsara go together—they imply one another. So you're only truly released if you see that—nirvana and birth and death are the same thing.

Every time an incarnation occurs, it feels like *this* one. We might be reincarnated in a different universe as beings of an altogether different shape, but that's the shape that feels normal—that's the shape that feels just as it feels to us to feel human. We're used to this shape, so it feels normal. If we were spiders, we'd look around at other spiders and think they were normal, but all other creatures would look unusual. Just imagine how we look to a fish—clumsy, cumbersome, and stupid looking, especially when we're attempting to swim. So, in every world that comes into being or *could* come into being, it seems just as this world seems right now, and every incarnation—no matter how strange from this vantage point—would feel just as this incarnation feels right now.

Every life form possesses some kind of awareness of superior and inferior forces. We humans generally aren't aware of species above us, unless we think we're in touch with angels or something of that sort. The things that seem superior to us are large natural processes like earthquakes or tiny organisms like viruses, although we don't attribute much intelligence to either. In any case, we feel we're in the middle. That is, we look through a telescope and consider cosmic realms infinitely greater than we are, and we look through the microscope to observe worlds infinitely smaller than we are, and we seem to stand somewhere in the middle of these two situations. But we're no more in the middle than any other creature. Anything with perception always perceives itself as somehow in the middle. Anything that grows anywhere is always in the middle. And the middle always has extremes—far west, far east; the top side, the bottom side; the beginning, the end.

So if you are aware of a state that you deem *reality* or *life*, this implies *illusion* or *unreality* or *death*. You can't know one without the other. And life isn't life without death—knowing that it will come to an end makes it poignant and *lively*. Liveliness is change and motion.

The only time you really feel a difference in your life is in moments of transition—things start to get better, and you feel great; things decline, and you get disappointed and gloomy. And you can go all the way down to death. It seems so final, irrevocable, and permanent, but what about the nothingness that went on before you were alive? This is what we've left out of our logic. We've hoodwinked ourselves by attributing powerlessness to nothingness. But just as you can't know form without the background, you can't know something—life—without nothing. You've heard the saying, "When you're dead, you're dead." The people who came up with that saying are the people who want to rule the world. They want to frighten you with the idea that death is final, that believing anything else is wishful thinking. They'll tell you to face the facts. What facts? How can I face the fact of "nothing," which, by definition, is not a fact? People who argue that the basic reality of all this is nothingness—physicists who think that the energy of the universe is gradually running down and dissipating, for example—ignore the fact that all of this comes from nothingness.

The sixth patriarch of Zen—Huineng, also known as Dajian—taught that the essence of our mind is intrinsically pure. He didn't mean "nondirty," but *clear* or *void*. He also taught that emptiness isn't blank but abundantly full, just as empty space is full of the whole universe—stars, moons, mountains, rivers, good people, evil people, animals, insects, and so on are all contained in the void. So, out of this void comes everything, and you're it. What else could you be?

What I'm illustrating is that all this fear of nothingness is just hocus-pocus. Nothingness is what we should be talking about more in spirituality, but people ignore it or put down that type of discussion. But that's where the secret lies. The secret always lies in the place where you don't look for it. Where was Christ the King born—in a palace? No. He was born where no one would think of looking—in a pigsty. So you should meditate on nothingness. I know it's difficult to think about, but it will be easier when you remember that nothingness is what you are and what you were before you were born. This is an extremely important point. It's the secret to the whole thing.

If you tell people this, they'll be sure to bug you about it. "In this philosophy of emptiness," they'll say, "there's no basis for loving other people, no basis for joy, no basis for cultivating anything good," and so on. Nonsense. If you truly explore nothingness, you'll become full of energy, so there's nothing in your way. And if that's the case, you can do this, that, and the other thing with glee and be thoroughly creative. Creativity requires nothingness, *real* nothingness—not some sort of darkness that resembles being buried alive forever. What is nothingness? It's beyond imagination. Your imagination exhausts itself trying to conceive of it.

This is what mystics have been talking about throughout history. *The Cloud of Unknowing*, written in the fourteenth century by an English monk, was based on an earlier text called *De Theologia Mystica* by a sixth-century Syrian monk who called himself Dionysius the Areopagite. It's a fascinating, short book that I translated back in 1943. It describes God entirely in negatives—not light, not power, not spirit, not father, not this, not that, not the other—the author simply negates anything anyone has ever said about God, because God is infinite and is therefore beyond the reach of all conception. "Anybody who, having a vision, thought he saw God, would not have seen God but some creature that God has made that is less than God," he writes. This is stated in such a way that even Saint Thomas of Aquinas bought it. Everybody's got to agree that God is the which of which there is no whicher, and Dionysius the Areopagite spells this out.

If you assert some idea of a tangible god, then you're stopping short. You don't get the whole benefit of this exploration. If you insist that there's something there—a loving father at the end of the line or some kind of garden paradise—you're really cheating yourself. You have to thoroughly explore emptiness or real downright nothingness, and that's what this whole Zen project, Vedanta, mysticism, and what-have-you are all about. And I think that's the simplest thing I can possibly tell you.

PART FOUR

THE WORLD

AS

JUST SO

10

The Koan of Zen

Lectures on Zen are a kind of hoax. Zen deals with the domain of experience that can't be talked about. For that matter, there's really nothing at all that can be adequately talked about. The whole art of poetry is to say what can't be said—every poet feels there's always something absolutely essential they're leaving out.

So Zen always describes itself as the finger pointing at the moon. In the Sanskrit saying *tat tvam asi*—"that art thou"—Zen concerns itself with "that." *That* is the word used for Brahman—the absolute reality in Hindu philosophy—and you're it, only in disguise, and disguised so well that even you've forgotten it. Zen takes these abstract ideas—Brahman, ultimate reality, the ultimate ground of being, the great self, the void, and so on—and concerns itself with a much more direct way of coming to an understanding of *that*. Here are four key phrases we can use to characterize Zen: direct transmission (beyond scriptures and tradition), beyond language, forthright pointing to the mind, and realizing one's own nature and becoming Buddha (waking up from the normal hypnosis under which almost all of us go around like somnambulists).

Why all this interest in Zen? I've wondered about this a lot, especially since much of this curiosity in the United States came after the war with Japan. First of all, I think the appeal of Zen lies in its unusual quality of humor. Religions aren't, as a rule, humorous in any way.

They are quite serious. But when one looks at Zen art or reads Zen stories, it's apparent that something is going on here that isn't serious in the ordinary sense, although it may be quite sincere. Second, I think another appeal to Westerners is the fact that Zen has no doctrines—there's nothing you have to believe—and Zen doesn't moralize at you very much. Zen isn't particularly concerned with morals at all. Zen is a field of inquiry like physics, and you wouldn't expect a physicist to be an authority on morals. You go to an ophthalmologist to have your eyes adjusted—Zen is like spiritual ophthalmology.

Another reason why Zen appeals to Western students is that they've received much of their understanding of Zen from D.T. Suzuki, R.H. Blyth, and me, and we present Zen in the form of Ch'an, specifically that which blossomed in China between 700 and 1000 CE. That differs greatly from the kind of Zen you'll find today in Japan, which makes a great fetish of studying Zen by sitting. R. H. Blyth asked one Zen master what he would do if he only had a half hour left to live. Would he listen to music? Get drunk? Take a walk? Enjoy the company of a beautiful woman? And the master just said, "Zazen"—that is, he'd choose to practice sitting meditation. Well, this answer bothered R. H. Blyth quite a bit, because he felt—as I do—that sitting is only one way of doing Zen. Buddhism refers to the four dignities of people—walking, standing, sitting, and lying—so there must also be walking Zen, standing Zen, and lying Zen. For example, you should also practice sleeping in a Zen way, which means sleeping thoroughly. This might sound similar to the old Western directive—"Whatever your hand finds to do, do it with all your might"—but that's not the same thing as Zen.

Paul Reps, who wrote a lovely book called *Zen Telegrams*, once asked a Zen master to sum up Buddhism in one phrase. The master said, "Don't act, but act." And this simply delighted Reps because this sounds a lot like the Taoist principle of *wu wei*—action in the spirit of not being separate from the world, realizing that your action is not an interference but an expression of the universe. But the master spoke terrible English, and Reps had misunderstood him. He actually said, "Don't act *bad* act." Well, this is the sort of attitude that *all* clergy develop over the centuries. You go to church, and the sermon boils down to this: *be good*. And everybody knows they should be good, but hardly anybody knows how. Or even what "being good" means.

So part of the fascination of Zen to the West is that it offers a sudden insight into something that was always supposed to take years and years and years to understand. Psychoanalysts will tell you that you can get straightened out, but only after countless sessions—maybe twice a week for several years. Christians will say that if you embark on a path of spiritual discipline and submit yourself to the will of God, you might attain the highest stages of contemplative prayer, but only after many years. And Buddhists will tell you that after many long years of meditation and stern discipline, you might make enough progress in this life to attain a better life in the next—perhaps as a monk—and that will get you into the preliminary states of Buddhahood, but it's all likely to take several incarnations to get there. But this isn't the case with Zen.

Zen literature abounds with dialogues—*mondo*, in Japanese—between Zen teachers and students. I gave a copy of one of these books, the *Mumonkan*—"the barrier with no gate" or "gateless gate"—to a friend of mine. He said, "I haven't understood a word of this, but it cheered me up enormously!" These dialogues between teachers and students are fascinatingly incomprehensible, and most end with the student getting the point. I say "students" instead of "monks" because in Zen you don't commonly take monastic vows for life regarding poverty, chastity, obedience, and so on. You're more like a student in a theological seminary who stays for a given amount of time and usually leaves, sometimes going into lay life or becoming a priest in charge of a temple. Regardless, you can still get married and have a family and so on. Only very few graduates of a Zen monastery become *roshis*, which means "old teachers." The roshi is in charge of the spiritual development of the students. One such student in the *Mumonkan* complains to the roshi that he has not received instruction, despite being at the monastery for some time. The master asks, "Have you had breakfast?" The student says, "Yes." The master replies, "Then go wash your bowl." And the student is awakened.

Now you might think that the moral of this story is to do the work at hand, or that the bowl is a symbol of the void. Or that because Zen monastics wash their bowl with tea immediately—and without prompting—after eating, the master was saying something like, "Don't gild the lily," or, to use a Zen phrase, "Don't put legs on a snake." But the point of the story is far more clear, and that's what's difficult about it. These stories resemble jokes in this way—a joke is told to make you laugh, and if you get the joke, you just laugh spontaneously. If the point of the joke has to be explained to you, however, it's not the same—you don't laugh so well, or maybe you fake a little laugh. These stories illustrate sudden insight into the nature of being, which is something you can't fake.

In another story, a master called Baijang had to choose a new master from among his students to run a particular monastery, so he designed a test. Baijang put down a picture in front of him and said, "Without making an assertion or denial, tell me what this is." The senior monk said, "It couldn't be called a piece of wood," but Baijang didn't accept the answer. Then the cook came forward, kicked the picture over, and walked away. Baijang gave him the job. And the commentary in the book says, "Maybe the cook wasn't so smart after all, for he gave up an easy job for a difficult one."

In yet another famous story, a master says, "When I was a young man and knew nothing of Buddhism, mountains were mountains and rivers were rivers. Then I began to understand a little about Buddhism, and mountains were no longer mountains and rivers were no longer rivers. And when I finally understood Buddhism thoroughly, mountains were mountains and rivers were rivers." In other words, once we start explaining things—for example, scientifically or philosophically—we see things as separate and causal, but if we look further, we see that there is nothing separate. Separation is an illusion, and this story points to that directly. Zen speaks of a virtue called *mushin* (which means "no mind") or *mumen* ("no thought"), but this doesn't mean that it is virtuous to be beyond any thought at all. What it means is not being fooled by thoughts—not being hypnotized by the forms of speech or images we place on the world, not confusing thoughts for the world itself.

There's a story that tells of Bodhidharma's visit with the Chinese emperor, Wu of Liang. The emperor was a great patron of Buddhism and announced to Bodhidharma, "We have built many monasteries, ordained countless monks and nuns, and translated the holy scriptures into Chinese. What is the merit of all of this?" And Bodhidharma said, "No merit whatsoever." This really shocked the emperor, because Buddhism teaches that such actions bring tremendous merit, which means a better rebirth, which means eventual liberation. So the emperor asked Bodhidharma, "Then what is the most important principle of the holy dharma?" And Bodhidharma answered, "Vast emptiness and nothing holy" or "In vast emptiness there is nothing holy." Again, taken aback, the emperor asked, "Well, then who is it that stands before us?" Bodhidharma responded, "I don't know." There's a famous poem that refers to this: "Plucking flowers to which the butterflies come, Bodhidharma says, 'I don't know.'" And another: "If you want to know where the flowers come from, even the God of spring doesn't know."

So anybody who says that they know what Zen is is a fraud. Nobody knows. Just like you don't know who you are—all this business about your name and accomplishments and certificates and what your friends say about you. You know very well that's not you. The problem of knowing who you are is the problem of smelling your own nose. And people who read about Zen in the West get this sense that perhaps the great understanding is right under their nose. It's like placing an absurd object in a room full of people—like a balloon on the ceiling. People enter the room and don't notice the balloon at all. Zen is exactly like that—it's very obvious. A student asked master Bokuju, "We have to get dressed and eat every day—how do we escape from it all?"—in other words, how do we get out of our routine—and Bokuju said, "We dress, we eat." The student said, "I don't understand," and Bokuju replied, "If you don't understand, put on your clothes and eat your food." A monk asked Joshu, "What is the way?"—the Tao, in Chinese. Joshu responded, "Your everyday mind is the way." "How do you get in accord with it?" the monk asked. Joshu replied, "When you try to accord, you deviate." All these stories are connected, and I want you to grasp the connection intuitively.

Having presented all these fireworks, let me say a few sober things about Zen as a historical phenomenon. Zen is a subdivision of Mahayana Buddhism, which is the school concerned with realizing Buddha Nature in this world—that is, not by renouncing family life and going off to meditate alone in the mountains. In other words, Zen comes from the style of Buddhism that doesn't see everyday life as an entanglement, but instead recognizes that one can become a Buddha in the midst of life. So the great personality in Mahayana Buddhism is the bodhisattva, someone who has attained nirvana but has chosen to come back again and again in various guises to help beings—Zen art sometimes presents bodhisattvas as prostitutes or bums. For example, the famous bum Hotei—Pu-Tai in Chinese—who is immensely fat, is shown, in a painting by Sengai, stretching and yawning as he wakes up, saying, "Buddha is dead. Maitreya [the next Buddha] hasn't come yet. I had a wonderful sleep and didn't even dream about Confucius."

So Zen is Indian Mahayana Buddhism translated into Chinese, which means it is deeply influenced by Taoism and Confucianism. The origins of Zen lie somewhere around 414 CE, at which time Kumarajiva, a great Hindu scholar, led the translation of Buddhist sutras into Chinese. Kumarajiva and his team of translators promoted enlightenment as a sudden event. That is, awakening happens instantaneously as an all-or-nothing event. As the analogy goes, when the bottom falls out of the bucket, all the water falls out.

Bodhidharma—the first Zen patriarch—came to China later; the second patriarch was a former army general named Eka; Sosan was the third patriarch—he authored the *Hsin-Hsin Ming*, a marvelous summary of Buddhism in verse. Then came Doshin—who reportedly attained enlightenment when he was fourteen years old—and Konin, who fully developed the East Mountain teachings. Finally, the sixth patriarch, Eno—most commonly known by his Chinese name, Huineng—is considered the real founder of Chinese Zen, the man who synthesized the whole thing, the teacher who really fused Zen with the Chinese way of doing things.

Huineng wrote the *Platform Sutra*, which any student of Zen should read. He famously said, "Do not think you are going to attain Buddhahood by sitting down all day and keeping your mind blank." That's what students of the time believed—that the proper way to contemplate was to be as still as possible—but according to the teachings, acting that way makes you a stone Buddha, not a living one. You can hit a stone Buddha over the head with a rock or break it into pieces, and it doesn't feel anything, and that's not the point. People who think that in order to be awakened you have to be heartless and beyond feelings—that you couldn't possibly lose your temper or feel annoyed or depressed—those people haven't got the right idea at all. And Eno—that is, Huineng—taught that: "If that's your ideal of enlightenment, you might as well be a block of wood or piece of stone."

What this means is that your real mind is imperturbable. When you move your hand through the air, it doesn't leave a track; when the water reflects the image of geese, the reflection doesn't stick. So, to be pure-minded in Zen—or, rather, "clear-minded" is a better way of translating it—means that your mind isn't sticky. You just go with the flow of life—you don't harbor grievances or remain stuck to the past. Life is flowing all the time—that's the Tao—and you're going to go along with the flow whether you want to or not. We're like people in a stream, and we can swim against the stream if we want, but all we'll do is wear ourselves out while the stream moves us along anyway. However, when we swim *with* the stream, the whole strength of the flow is ours. Of course, the difficulty that many of us have is finding out which way the stream is going.

Eno died in 713 CE and left behind five great disciples who taught this same sort of thing. But as things go, these five disciples had their disciples, and those disciples had their disciples, and so on and so on. So in Zen you have what are called "houses"—some of them died out, some continue to this day. And today Zen lives on in two forms—Rinzai and Soto, each with a different emphasis. Soto people tend to be more serene in their approach, whereas Rinzai is more gutsy—it's the mainly Rinzai people who use koan practice.

The period between Eno's death and 1000 CE is considered the golden age of Zen. After this period, Zen declined in China and got mixed up with Taoist alchemy and other forms of Buddhism, namely those that stress *siddhis*—supernormal powers. But this is all completely beside the point in Zen. However, a very strong strain of Zen went to Japan with Eisai in 1191 CE and Dogen in around 1227 CE. Before this time, however—that is, in the golden age—the main practice of Chinese Zen was walking, as opposed to sitting. Zen monks were great travelers—they walked for miles and miles across all types of terrain to visit temples in order to encounter masters who could cause their spark to flash. In Japanese this is called *satori*, in Mandarin *wu*, and in Cantonese *hoi ng*. It means "awakening" in the same way that *bodhi* in Sanskrit alludes to awakening from the illusion of being a separate ego locked up in a bag of skin. In other words, you discover you are the whole universe, and you discover it suddenly, which is a shock—your common sense is turned directly inside out. Everything is the same as it was before, only completely different, because you now know who you are. What the devil were you worrying about before? What was all that fuss and to-do about? Well, you see, it was part of the game. From one point of view, it's all fuss and to-do, to-do, to-do. But when you wake up, you discover that the to-do wasn't you—it was the entire works, the *it*. And you are it, and it is it, and everything is it, and it does all things that are done.

11

Nonduality in Action

I want to talk now about an aspect of Zen practice called "going straight ahead." A student once asked his master, "What is the Tao?"—that is, "What is the way?"—and the master replied, "Walk on." Today we would say, "Go!"—as in, "Go, man, go!" This aspect of Zen refers to detachment—having a mind that isn't sticky or one that doesn't fumble, wobble, or hesitate. When Zen teachers ask students a question, they expect an immediate answer, one without premeditation or deliberation. In Zen, they speak of a kind of person who "doesn't depend on anything." This means a person who doesn't rely on formulas, theories, or beliefs to govern their actions.

It's very difficult for us to function this way. We've been brought up to believe that there are two sides to ourselves: an animal side and a human—that is to say, civilized—side. Freud referred to these as the side of the pleasure principle/animal nature/id and the reality principle/social nature/superego; and in his view, these two sides of a person are in constant battle. Theosophists speak of a higher, spiritual self and a lower, psychic (ego-oriented) self. And if you look at things in this way, the problem of life is to make your better self take charge of your lower self—like a rider taking charge of a horse. But here's the real problem: How would you know if what you think is your higher self isn't really your lower self in disguise? When a thief robs a house and the cops get called, they enter the house on the ground floor while the thief climbs the stairs to the next floor up. And when the police go up to that floor, the thief climbs up to the next. In the same way, when we feel ourselves to be the lower self—that is, a separate ego—the moralists come along and say, "Don't be selfish," so the ego tries to pretend it's good by identifying with a higher self.

Why do you believe you have a higher self? Have you seen it? Do you know that it's there? No. You just want to do your duty or behave like a proper member of society. But that's all a great phony front. If you don't know there's a higher self, and you believe that there is one, on whose authority do you believe this? Buddhists might cite the Buddha, Hindus might say the Upanishads, Christians will say Jesus. The Baltimore Catechism begins, "We are bound to believe that there is but one God, the Father Almighty, Creator of Heaven and Earth," and Catholics look down upon Protestants for interpreting the Bible however they'd like without any authoritative version. But this ignores the fact that Catholics choose to accept the authority of the church to interpret the Bible for them. In other words, it must become clear to you that you yourself create all the authorities you accept. Otherwise, the whole thing is phony.

Zen doesn't present a duality between a higher and lower self. If you believe in the higher self, it's just a simple trick of the lower self. If you believe there is no lower self, but only the higher self, or that the lower self is merely something for the higher self to shine through, that's just lending validity to the duality. If you think you have a lower self—or an ego to get rid of—and you fight against it, nothing strengthens the delusion that it exists more than that. So this tremendous schizophrenia in humans—of thinking they are rider and horse, soul in command of body, a will that must control passions, and so on—this kind of split thinking simply aggravates the problem. We just get more and more split. Thinking this way just results in an interior conflict that will never, never get resolved. You either know the true self or you don't, and if you do know it, then this thing we call the lower self ceases to be a problem, because it's just a mirage. Well, you don't go around hitting at mirages with a stick or trying to put reins on them. You just know they're mirages and walk right through them.

When I was a child and did naughty things, my mother would say, "Alan, that's not like you." So I gained a conception of what *was* like me in my better moments—that is to say, the moments when I remembered what my mother would like me to do. That's the kind of split that's implanted in us all. And because we're split-minded, we're always dithering—Is the choice I'm about to make from the higher self or the lower self? Is it of the spirit or of the flesh? Is the message I received from God or the Devil? And nobody can decide, because if you knew how to choose, you wouldn't have to. You can think about it until you're blue, but you'll never get the answer, because the problems of life are so subtle that to try to solve them with vague principles—even if those vague principles come in the form of specific moral instructions—is completely impossible.

So it's important to overcome split-mindedness. But how? Where do you start if you're already split? One Taoist aphorism says, "When the wrong man uses the right means, the right means work in the wrong way." So what are you to do? How can you get moving? Fundamentally, of course, you have to be surprised into it.

Winthrop Sargeant once interviewed a great Zen priest in Kyoto. The priest asked, "Who are you?" to which Winthrop Sargeant replied, "I'm Winthrop Sargeant." And the priest laughed. "No," he said, "I don't mean that. I mean, who are you, really?" Well, this led to Sargeant putting forth all sorts of abstractions about his being a particular human being—a journalist and musician and so on—and the priest just kept laughing. Eventually, the priest moved on to other topics, Sargeant relaxed, and the priest eventually made some little joke, and Sargeant laughed. And the priest said, "*There* you are!"

See, that laughter wasn't a deliberate response. A response of a non-deliberating mind is a response of a Buddha mind, or an unattached mind. But this is not the same as a quick response, because if you get hung up on the idea of responding quickly, the idea of quickness becomes a form of obstruction. Sometimes Dr. Suzuki would respond to questions after a full minute of silence, but it was still a spontaneous response, because during the silence, he wasn't fishing around to think of something to say—he wasn't embarrassed by the silence or by not knowing the answer. If you don't know the answer, you can be silent. If nobody asks a question, you can be silent. There's no need to be embarrassed about it or get stuck on it. But you also can't overcome being stuck if you think that somehow you would be guilty if you *were* stuck. When you are perfectly free to feel stuck or not stuck, then you're unstuck. Nothing can stick to the real mind—you'll find this out yourself if you watch the flow of your thoughts.

What we call "stream of consciousness" or "flow of thoughts" is described in Chinese by repeating the character for "thought" three times—*nian, nian, nian*. Thought, thought, thought. When you ruminate, thought follows thought—thoughts rise and fall like waves on the water. And when thoughts fall away, it is as if they had never been. When you see this, you'll see that your mind doesn't really stick—it's just that you get the illusion of it sticking. You might experience a cycle of the same succession of thoughts that gives you some sense of permanence, but it's just an illusion. It's from our connecting thoughts together that we get the sensation that behind our thoughts there is a thinker who controls the thoughts and experiences them. But the notion that there is a thinker is just a thought in the stream of thoughts—thought, thought, thought, thinker, thought, thought, thinker, thought, thought, thought, thinker, and so on. And if this happens regularly enough, you get the illusion of there being someone who thinks apart from the stream of thoughts which come and go.

So that's how we become split-minded. We think there is some real entity that stands aside from thoughts and chooses among them, controls them, regulates them, and so on. Actually, this is a way to *not* be able to control one's thoughts. The stronger the duality between thinker and thoughts and feeler and feelings, the more the stream of sensations is coaxed into self-protective activity. It becomes more and more like a stuck record in order to protect and aggrandize and enlarge the status of the supposed thinker.

If I say, "Walk or sit, but whatever you do, don't wobble," what am I saying? What kind of statement is that? When I raise that question—that is, *What kind of statement is that?*—I'm beginning to talk about talking. And I can do that, provided I don't try to do so while making the original statement. If I want to say something about what I just said, I must do it later, correct? But not at the same time. I cannot say you are a fool while simultaneously saying, "And now I'm giving you an insult," in so many words—not unless I invent an exceedingly complex language that talks about itself as it goes along. I'm explaining this to illustrate how we get completely mixed up. In the middle of being about to express something, we start thinking about whether it is the right or best thing to say—in other words, we start wobbling. We start to get too much feedback, and too much feedback makes any mechanism go crazy. And when you become very aware of a difference between the deeds and the doer, and the doer is commenting on the deeds while doing them, the doer never really gets with it. You try to strike a nail with a hammer, and just as you're about to hit the nail, you wonder if it's the best place to put it. That's why you probably hit your thumb—you didn't go right through with hitting the nail.

I'm not saying that there should be no criticism of thought. I'm saying that when you criticize thought *while* you're thinking, it makes you balled up and fundamentally confused. That's what's meant by the Sanskrit term *klesha*—a disturbing confusion of the mind. And this kind of confusion is particular to humans because we have language, and I use that word very inclusively—words, images, numbers, notations, and so on. So because we can talk about anything, we can talk about talking, we can talk about thinking, and we can talk about ourselves as if we could stand to the side and say, "Said I to myself, said I." But all we are actually doing is making a second thought that comments on the previous one while pretending that the second thought is a different one from the first. And we buy this because we believe all kinds of phony images about memory—for example, we think of memory in terms of engraving, as if we employed a flat and stable surface upon which to make marks that stay there for future review. We think that there is something stable upon which the passage of thoughts makes an impression.

Does this sound familiar? This idea is directly related to the ancient superstition that the world consists of two elements—stuff and form. This is the ceramic model of the universe. God formed Adam out of the dust of the ground. So there is stuff on one side and form engraved upon it—imposed upon it, stamped upon it—like a seal stamped on wax. But what is stuff like apart from form? And what is form like apart from stuff? Nobody has ever seen a piece of shapeless stuff, and nobody has ever seen a piece of stuffless shape—they're the same thing. It isn't necessary to think of them as different.

There is process. There is the flow of thought. The flow of thought doesn't have to happen to someone. Experience doesn't have to beat upon some experiencer. It's just a stream happening that we convince ourselves that we stand to the side of and observe, because that's how we've been brought up. In my thought and experience, *I* am an object—a very fleeting and passing one—and *you* are an object, one that comes and goes. I think there is a *me* surrounded by an external world, and you think the same. But if you really think about that—that I am in your external world and you are in my external world—you will realize it is all one world that goes along together. There's no such thing as *internal* or *external*—it's all simply the process. So it's important to get rid of the illusion of duality between the thinker and the thought. Find out who the thinker is—the one who seems to be behind the thoughts. Who is the real, genuine you?

Zen masters sometimes use shouting as a method. The master says, "I want to hear you say the word *mo* and really mean it. I want to hear not just the sound, but the person who says it. Now, produce that for me." And the student shouts, "Mo!" And the Zen teacher says, "Nope. That's not it." And the student yells, "Mo!" even louder, and the master says, "Not quite. It's still coming from your throat." And this goes on for a long time, because the true mo will never come while the student is still making a differentiation between a true mo and a false mo.

To act with confidence, you just do it. But people aren't used to that, so it's necessary to set up protected situations like the one above in which it can be done. If we acted without deliberation in the ordinary way of social intercourse, we would get into amazing confusions. If we actually followed our parents' advice to always tell the truth, for example, and we said what we truly thought about other people, we'd likely get in a great deal of trouble. But Zen offers a kind of enclosure within which to practice this sort of behavior—and people get expert in it and learn how to apply it in all situations. Zen teachers put their students in the types of situations that would result in them getting stuck in the normal course of social relations. For example, they ask nonsensical questions like, "What is the sound of one hand clapping?" and make impossible demands such as, "Touch the ceiling without getting up from your chair" or "Stop the sound of that train whistle." And when we interpret these questions or demands in an ordinary way, they're impossible. We have to go beyond our particular means of discourse.

All these games we play—social games, production games, survival games—are good games. But we take them too seriously. We think that the *I* is the only important thing; so Zen works to unstick us from that notion, and in doing so, we realize that it would be just as good a game to drop dead now as it would be to go on living. Is a lightning flash bad because it only lasts a split second? Is a star good because it exists for billions of years? You can't make that sort of comparison. A world of lightning goes with a universe full of stars—short-lived and long-lived creatures go together. That's the meaning of the poem, "Flowering branches grow naturally—some short, some long."

In a Zen community, spontaneous behavior is encouraged within certain limits, and as the student becomes more and more used to it, those limits are expanded. Eventually, the student can go out on the street and behave like a true Zen character and get by perfectly well. You know how you encounter someone on the street—you're walking straight toward each other and you both decide to move in the same direction to avoid one another, and then you both move back in the other direction, and you get closer and closer to colliding? That's the kind of trick that Zen teachers pull on their students. They get the student all tangled up to see how they escape from it.

In everyday life, there's a very clear distinction between people who always seem to be self-possessed and people who are dithering and nervous. The latter don't quite know how to react in any given situation—they're always getting embarrassed because their life is too strongly programmed. "You said you would do such and such a thing at such and such a time, and now you've changed your plans and messed up everything"—isn't this a common marriage argument? The change of plans doesn't actually cause any significant inconvenience—it's just a feeling that comes from being very inadaptable. If it doesn't particularly matter when we do such and such a thing, and somebody gets offended because the time gets changed, that's simply because they are attached to punctuality as a fetish. We spend an awful lot of energy trying to make our lives fit images of what life is or should be—images which our lives could never possibly match or fit. So Zen practice entails getting rid of these images.

In our culture, we have people who are comedians—they know how to make jokes and pull off gags in completely unprepared situations. Well, a Zen master does the very same thing in everyday situations. You can do this, too, as long as you remember one thing, and it's a secret—you cannot make a mistake. That's a very difficult thing to understand. Since childhood, we've conformed to a certain social game that says you mustn't make mistakes, you must do the right thing, you must enact a certain appropriate behavior here and certain appropriate behavior there, and so on. Well, that really sticks with us—it's hard to grow out of that childhood game. Similarly, we still believe the childhood game that says there are three kinds of people: top, middle, and bottom. Everybody wants to be the top set of people—they live up the hill, drive Cadillacs, have nice wall-to-wall carpeting, mowed lawns, and all those sorts of things. And nobody wants to be the bottom set of people who live near the waterfront, grow beards, wear blue jeans, and smoke marijuana. Most of us are somewhere in the middle, and we're always trying to climb our way up, never realizing that the top needs the bottom and the bottom needs the top.

This competition game shows up in other ways, too—I'm stronger than you; I'm smarter than you; I'm more loving than you; I'm more tolerant than you; I'm more sophisticated than you; and so on. It doesn't matter what it is—this status game is always going on. Well, a Zen student is a person who has stopped playing the status game. The real meaning of being a monk is no longer trying to keep up with the Joneses. To become a master he or she must get to the point where they're not trying to become a master. The whole idea of being better than someone else doesn't make any sense at all. It's totally meaningless. See, everyone is manifesting the marvel of the universe in the same way as the stars, water, wind, and animals do. And you see them all as being in their right places and not being able to make mistakes, really, even if *they* think in their own way that they're making mistakes and playing their own type of competitive game.

So if the game begins to bore you or give you trouble and ulcers, then you might think about quitting the game and become interested in something like Zen. But that's simply a symptom of you growing in a certain direction. When you are tired of playing a certain kind of game, you are as naturally flowing in another direction as a tree that puts out a new branch. And hopefully you do so beyond the distinctions of superior and inferior—that is, you don't think, "I'm a spiritual person now who attends to higher things; I'm not one of these morons who is just interested in beer and television." There are various ways to live life, just as there are crabs and spiders and sharks and sparrows and so on. Remember the poem I quoted earlier that says, "Flowering branches grow naturally—some short, some long"? The first verse of the same poem reads, "In the landscape of spring, there is nothing superior and nothing inferior." What is the point in superiority? In the process of growth, the oak is not better than the acorn. The oak is just an acorn's way of becoming more acorns.

So there's a particular benefit to becoming an outcaste in the sense of no longer taking the social game seriously. And even when people are constantly yammering and yammering at you to play the game, you don't feel threatened by the idea of making mistakes, or doing the wrong thing. In other words, you move beyond carrying your childhood conditioning into adulthood. Preachers and judges and teachers of all types take the same attitude toward adults that parents take toward children—they lecture them as to what they should and should not do. Well, maybe some criminals have yet to grow up, but you could say the same for judges—it takes two to make a quarrel. And when you leave the game, you can start thinking in a new way—in polarities as opposed to conflicts—because you no longer need to be stuck with competitive thinking: good guys versus bad guys, cops versus robbers, capitalists versus communists, and all these other ideas that are simply childish.

Of course, I'm using a type of competitive language to show that the competitive game has limitations. It's like I just said, "Look, I have something to tell you, and if you get it, you'll be in a much better position than you were before you heard what I'm about to say." But you can't speak to a particular group without using the language, gestures, customs, and what-have-you of that group. And Zen masters try to get around this situation by acting in strange and sudden ways that people just can't grasp. That's the real reason why Zen can't be explained. You have to make a jump from the valuation game—better versus worse people, in-group versus out-group, and so forth—and you can only make this jump by seeing that they are all mutually interdependent. So let's say I'm talking to you, and I say, "Look, I have a very special thing to tell you that you absolutely need to pay attention to." Well, I'm the in-group and you're the out-group. But really, I can't play the teacher unless you play the student or listener—my status and position are totally dependent on you. It's not something I have first, and then you get—these things arise mutually. So if you didn't listen to what I have to say, I wouldn't talk. I wouldn't know what to say.

So that's the insight that things go together. And when you see that and are no longer in competition, you don't make mistakes, because you don't dither. When I first learned to play the piano, my teacher hit my fingers with a pencil every time I played a wrong note. Consequently, I never learned to read music—I was afraid of that pencil, so I hesitated too long. That kind of thing gets built into our psyches. Even though we're adults and beyond being beaten or screamed at, we still hear the echoes in the back of our heads of Mama yelling or Papa shouting. And we pass the same attitudes to our own children, and the farce just continues. That isn't to say you shouldn't lay down the law with your children, but you should make some kind of provision for later in life to liberate them—I mean, you should go through some process of curing them from the bad effects of education. But you can't do that unless you grow up, too. Unless *we* grow up. I should include myself in that statement.

When we first encounter Zen masters, they initially come across as extremely authoritarian figures. That is, they put on a terrific show of being an awful dragon, because this screens out people who don't have the nerve to get into the work. But once you make it past this, a very interesting change takes place. The master becomes more like a brother or sister. They become an affectionate helper, and the students love the master as they would a close sibling, as opposed to respecting the master as they would a parent. And the students and masters make jokes about each other—they enjoy a very curious kind of social relationship. It has all the outward trappings of being authoritarian, but everybody on the inside knows what a joke this is. See, liberated people have to be very cool. Otherwise, a society that doesn't really believe in equality and can't possibly practice it would consider this kind of relationship a threat. It would be viewed as extremely subversive. So Zen masters wear all this purple and gold and carry scepters and sit on thrones. The outside world looks at that and thinks, "Okay, they're all right. They have discipline and order, so they must be fine."

12

A Great Doubt

Since I've discussed its basic principles, I'd like to convey the more practical side of Zen. A typical Zen institution consists of a campus with several buildings, and around the edges of the campus, you'll find temples founded in times past by noble families. When the Buddhists came East, they exploited ancestor worship—the great religion of China—which was very clever of them. Buddhist priests offered services like requiem masses for the repose of souls and ceremonies for good reincarnations of one's ancestors. So one of the principal functions of temples in Japan is to hold memorial services for the departed. People in Japan don't go to temple in the same way as Westerners go to church—they make pilgrimages and chant and attend special services like memorials and weddings, but they don't participate regularly in a parish kind of community. Of course, this began to look different in the United States among Japanese immigrants, many of whom copied practices of the Protestants. And a lot of the children these days don't understand Japanese and can't stand sutra chanting.

In Japan, the temples are run by priests and their families, and many of them have started to struggle. So to make a go of it, they add restaurants with very elegant food or museums. The guts of a Zen temple is what's called a *sodo—so* means the "sangha" and *do* means "hall." So the sangha hall is at the center of everything. This hall has a number of rooms, but the main one—the actual sodo—is a long, spacious room with platforms on either side and a wide passage down the center. The platforms are six feet wide, and each contains a number of tatami mats that measure six by three, and every monk is assigned to a mat upon which they sleep and meditate. On a shelf against the wall, the monks keep all their possessions, which are very simple. In the center of the passage between the platforms, you'll find an image of the bodhisattva Manjushri—called Monju in Japan—who holds the sword of *prajna* ("wisdom") that cuts asunder all illusions. And the hall has a kitchen and a library and other rooms for special services. There's also the quarters of the *kansho*—the abbot and administrative head of the temple—and the roshi. Each temple is somewhat independent, particularly in Rinzai Zen. That is, there's a fraternal relationship among all the temples—there's nothing like a pope or an archbishop or any hierarchy of that sort. The Soto sect has a little bit more of that, but on the whole, you could say that in Zen the kansho is the big boss of each temple, whereas the roshi is the respected boss—the man everybody's terrified of, at least on the outside.

If you want to study Zen at one of these institutions, they make it difficult. They actually try to repel you. So that's another difference from the welcome attitude you get at most Christian churches. The formal approach entails the prospective student arriving at the gate of the temple in traditional traveling gear—enormous straw hat, black robe, white *tabi* socks, and particular wooden sandals. The would-be student also carries a little box containing eating bowls, toothbrush, razor, and other necessities of life. And when the student arrives, they're told that the monastery is very poor, that they can't afford to bring in any more students, that the teacher is getting old and feeble, and other things like that. So the student has to remain outside and wait, but they're invited in for meals, because no traveling monk can be refused hospitality. And at night, the student is brought into a special room where they are expected to remain awake and spend all night in meditation. Back in the old days, this process might go on for a week or more so that the student could be thoroughly tested.

If the student makes it this long, they'll be invited to speak with the roshi. Now remember: from the outside, the roshis are formidable fellows—they possess a certain fierceness coupled with tremendous directness. In other words, the roshi is somebody who sees right through you. So when the student meets the roshi, the master right away poses a question like, "What do you want?" or "Why did you come here?" And the student, of course, announces that they have come to study Zen, to which the teacher responds, "We don't teach anything here. There isn't anything in Zen to study." And if the student is sharp enough, they will understand that this "not anything" is the real thing—the universe, the void, *shunyata*—so they're not fazed by the roshi's response. At this point, if the student insists that they wish to stay at the temple anyway to work and meditate and so on, they will likely be accepted on probation.

The preliminary interview can go on for some time after this. The teacher might pose the question, "Now, why do you want to study Zen?" And the student's response to this is something like, "Because I'm oppressed by the rounds of birth and death—the cycle of suffering. I want to be free." And the teacher asks, "Who is it that wants to be free?" And that's a stopper—the student's first koan. Or the interview might begin more casually with the master asking questions about the student's hometown, family, education, and so on. But in the middle of these seemingly relaxed questions, the roshi drops the koan—something like, "Why is my hand so much like the Buddha's hand?" And the student is blocked. The word *koan* actually means "a case"—as in a case of law, something that functions as a precedent for future cases. Most koans are based on stories of conversations between the old masters and their students, but some can arise spontaneously. The basic koan, however, is always, "Who are you?" And the roshi won't take words for an answer.

After this interview, the student goes to the chief monk—the *jikijitsu*—and learns what the rules are, where to sleep, how to meditate, and so on. The monks sit on padded cushions, their legs in the lotus posture for half-hour periods. When the time is up, they all get up and walk around the room briskly for a while until they're given the signal to sit down, at which point they go back to meditating. And during this routine, there's a monk on each side of the room who carries a long flat stick, and if they see a monk who's slouching or sleeping or goofing off in some way, they whack that monk on the back of the shoulders with this stick. Now, some apologists will tell you that this isn't punishment, that the whack is just to help the monks stay awake, but don't you believe it. Zen people are cool about it, but it's actually a fierce thing.

When you first begin zazen—that is, sitting meditation—you don't do much other than count your breathing, maybe by tens, until your thoughts become more still. And Zen people don't close their eyes when they meditate, nor do they close their ears. They keep their eyes on the floor in front of them, and they don't try to force away any sounds that are going on or any smells or any other sensations whatsoever. They don't block any of that out. And as time goes on, they spend less time counting their breath and more time devoted to the koan assigned to them by the roshi—*What is the sound of one hand clapping? Who were you before your father and mother conceived you? Does a dog have Buddha Nature?* That sort of thing.

Every day the student goes to the teacher for what is called *sanzen*—the study of Zen—to present an answer to the koan. There's a very formal approach to this meeting: the monk stops outside the master's quarters, hits a drum three times; the master replies with a bell, and the student goes in, bows, and repeats the koan aloud. Then they give their answer. Well, if the master isn't satisfied with the answer, he or she may simply ring the bell, which means, "interview over." Or the roshi might puzzle the student further—push them along in one direction or the other. Can you tell what's going on here? The student is being asked to be absolutely genuine, which you can't do on command—especially when the person you're confronted with is this authority figure, even more powerful and respected than your own father (which is saying a lot in Japan). So you're asked to be completely spontaneous in the presence of this tiger. And as your answers to the koan are rejected over and over, you become more desperate and experience a state known as the "great doubt." At this point, a student will try anything—there are even stories of them hitting their teacher with a rock—but nothing will do. A friend of mine who was studying in Kyoto once pulled a bullfrog out of his kimono in desperation. And the master just shook his head and said, "Too intellectual." He meant too contrived, too premeditated. My friend was just copying other people's Zen antics, and that's something you just can't get away with.

This desperation can become critical during *sesshin*—an intense period of practice in which the monks only sleep four hours a night, meditate all day, and go for their sanzen interview twice a day. It's a tremendous workout—usually five or six days long—and people get worked into a pitch of psychic fury. And during this intensification, the usual way of doing things gets exhausted. The student goes before the master and just stops giving a damn, because they've seen the point—there was never a problem to begin with. The student made up the problem. The student made up the problem and projected it on the master, who knew how to handle the whole situation, mainly by making the student much more stupid than they were before. This is how the student finally comes to see the essential stupidity of the human situation where we are playing a game of one-upping other people and the universe.

Who said you could get the better of life? What makes you think you're separate from life? How can you beat the game? What game? This illusion of beating the game is dissipated by the koan. They say that working on a koan is like a mosquito biting an iron bull—it's the nature of a mosquito to bite, but it's the nature of an iron bull to remain unbitten.

Now, once the roshi accepts the student's answer to the koan, the whole thing continues. There are five classes of koans, and this was just the first step, so the master encourages the student to redouble their efforts. The first koan was a Hinayana case—one meant to help the student reach nirvana—but the other four classes of koans are from the Mahayana and are therefore intended to bring nirvana into the world. So these koans have to do with miracles—for example, blowing out a candle in faraway Timbuktu—and how Zen understands dealing with various problems of the world. Now, this all takes differing periods of time. For some people, it only takes ten years. And on the day of graduation, everybody turns out and there's a great hullabaloo and they salute the departing monk, who goes out to become a layperson, or maybe a temple priest, or even one day a roshi.

So the whole system is homeopathic. It uses the hair of the dog that bit you as the cure for the bite. When people are deluded, they cannot be talked out of their delusion. No amount of talk could persuade anybody that the ego is an illusion—we *know* it's there. So the only way to convince a fool of their folly is to make them go further into it, just as William Blake says: "The fool who persists in his folly will become wise." Some psychiatrists I know have tried this method—making an overeater who is tremendously fat put on fifteen more pounds, for example, or getting an alcoholic terribly drunk and sick—but it's a rather desperate method. It's a rather dangerous method, too. Without a good adviser, people could easily go crazy under the strain.

So this method of Zen training only works for someone who will be satisfied by nothing else in the world—they just *have* to do it. And that's why this method isn't suitable for the modern age, and why most Japanese temples are relatively empty. In fact, most temples that have remained open have become old and set in their ways—they're very fixed and traditional, and a lot of what they do is meaningless. Zen is certainly not going to last in that form. It's even common—and has been since the time of Hakuin—for masters to expect students to answer koans in a prescribed way with fixed answers. After they give the right answer, students read a little book of poetry called the *Zenrin Kushu*—the Zen Forest Anthology—to find the meaning of their koan. Recently, this bothered a monk who threatened to publish all the answers to the koans so the masters would have to get on their toes and invent new ones. I know a roshi who invents new koans on the spot. When a student begins to answer, as soon as they open their mouth, the roshi says, "No! Too late!"

Part of the problem modern Zen has is one of archaic language. I mean, who wants to know about Joshu's *mo* anymore, or the sound of one hand clapping? Well, if you are versed in Chinese, there's a proverb that states, "One hand won't make a clap," so that koan makes sense to you. All these old stories and dialogues are full of references and allusions that don't exactly fit the world of today, so there's a need for modernization—referencing things that are going on *now*. There's a history of breaking from tradition in Japan—the seventeenth century was a great time of cultural democratization. For example, it's when Basho invented the haiku form of poetry. Before that, poetry was obscure and effete, and you had to be of the sophisticated literati to write it, but Basho's new form made it possible for everybody. People no longer thought of poetry as something that required publication—they now wrote poems at parties. And all this came out of Basho's Zen feeling for nature—short, insightful glimpses into nature—and Basho thought this should be within everybody's reach.

At the same time that Basho was taking poetry to the peasants, a man named Bankei began presenting Zen to farmers. Bankei offered an entirely different system of Zen, which he called *fu-sho*. Fu-sho means the "unborn"—that which has not yet arisen and, as a matter of fact, never does arise. Bankei asserted that we receive an immortal, unborn mind—the Buddha mind—from our parents, that *everyone* possesses it, and that it's all we need to face whatever we meet in life. As one interesting proof, he offered the fact that when we hear a variety of sounds—for example, if we're in a forest surrounded by the calls of crows and sparrows and so on—we hear each sound distinctly without any special effort on our parts. How can such an amazing thing happen so naturally? This ability comes from the Buddha mind, which is unborn, and therefore immortal.

There's a story of a priest coming to Bankei and saying, "Well, what you teach sounds great, but when I get in touch with my Buddha mind, I just get absentminded." Bankei responded by pointing out that if he were to stab the priest in the back with something sharp, the priest would feel the pain acutely, thereby proving that his mind was quite alert. And there's another example of a layperson complaining to Bankei about their own laziness, their weariness of Zen discipline, and their inability to advance along the path. Bankei replied, "Nonsense. When you're in the Buddha mind, there's no need to advance, and it's impossible to backslide. When you understand this point, you'll no longer bother yourself with silly concerns like that." You see, Bankei taught that thoughts arise from the shallow parts of one's mind, and because thoughts aren't actual entities, all you really have to do is let them come up, hang out for a while, and disappear. Thoughts just naturally come and go like that. We only go astray when we get hung up on them.

So Bankei's primary instruction was to let that natural process happen. He said that if you let thoughts come and go, you'll stay in the Buddha mind, and therefore, practicing things like discipline and zazen isn't really that important. "The birthless Buddha mind," he said, "has absolutely nothing to do with sitting with an incense stick in front of you. Whether awake or asleep, one is a living Buddha." And so Bankei attempted a Zen of no methods—you could meditate if you wanted to, but it wasn't necessary. He taught that meditating in order to become enlightened is like trying to make a mirror by polishing a brick. He also said that trying to purify your mind is like trying to wash blood off with more blood.

Bankei was the abbot of Myoshin-ji, where he stopped the practice of hitting sleeping monks with the *kaiseki* stick, because, he said, "A sleeping man is still a Buddha, and you shouldn't be disrespectful." Hakuin—his contemporary—had eighty successors, but Bankei had none. And some people think that was the most admirable thing about him.

PART FIVE

THE WORLD
AS
SELF

13

Hindu Cosmology

The Upanishads are the distilled essence of Hindu thought. In them, we learn the basis of all Indian philosophy—the "atman" in Sanskrit, or "self" in English. However, this is the "self" in the vastest and most inclusive sense of the word—*your* self, the *self as such, existence as such*, the *totality of all being*.

Of course, this is something that one cannot talk about logically. I mean, you can talk about it, just as a poet can talk about anything, and the Upanishads are mostly poetry. Of course, everything in the world—knives, forks, tables, trees, and stones—is indescribable. Twentieth-century scholar Alfred Korzybski referred to the physical world as the "unspeakable world," which is rather funny in that it means two things. First, you can't say anything about the physical world—it's ineffable; second, the physical world is something *not* to be spoken of—it's taboo, as we'll examine further. But from the standpoint of logic, we can't say anything about everything, because in order to do so in logical fashion, you must classify the item under discussion. Now, classes are intellectual boxes—for example, the three boxes of the game animal-vegetable-mineral. You can't know one classification without another. In order to have a box, you must have something inside the box and that which lies outside the box, and by this method of contrast, we can have a logical discussion about things. All words, therefore, are labels—intellectual pigeonholes.

But when you examine what fundamentally *is*, you're beyond the scope of boxes, and you can no longer speak logically. Of course, you can distinguish *is* from *is not*, but only in a very limited way. You could, for example, say, "I have a pen in my left hand, I do not have a pen in my right hand," and from this you could abstract the idea of *to be* and *not to be*, or *is* and *isn't*. However, when we consider *being* with a capital *B,* it includes examples of *is* such as celestial bodies, but it also entails examples of *isn't* such as the space that encompasses those celestial bodies, and these two things go together.

A perfectly logical person would say that the notion of the self—the atman, the fundamental reality in which everything exists—is meaningless. From a logical point of view, it is. However, just because something cannot be placed into a logical category doesn't indicate that it isn't real. The self bears somewhat the same relationship to the world as the diaphragm of a stereo speaker—none of the music that comes out of the speaker is about the diaphragm and nobody talks about the diaphragm, but the diaphragm makes it all happen. Everything you hear out of the speaker—all these different sounds and noises—are vibrations of this metallic device. It's the same with your eardrum or visual apparatus. Just as we might ask, "What's it on?" when talking about music—that is, tape, vinyl, and so on—the Hindus would respond, "It's on the self."

It isn't that there's only one self in a solipsistic way. Solipsism is the idea that you are the only person who exists and everybody else is your dream. Nobody can prove that this isn't the case, but I'd like to see a congress of solipsists arguing as to which one of them is really there. No, the atman is more complex than that. Think of the nerves in your body—there are billions and billions of them. Now imagine that at the end of each nerve is a little eye that gets impressions of the world and sends the information back to the central brain. This is more like the Hindu idea. Each person, animal, rock, blade of grass, and so on is an eye that looks out of one central self. Well, it is easy to see the connection between a single nerve and the brain, but it is much more difficult to see the connection between one individual human and another. We're not rooted to the same ground like trees, so it's easy for me to form the impression that I am only what is inside my bag of skin and that my self is a different self from your self—in other words, it seems like we're fundamentally disconnected.

However, in Hindu thought, each one of us is the works. That's a startling point of view. And the Hindus say that the self—the great self—is consciousness, but not ordinary everyday consciousness. Of course, everyday consciousness is a manifestation of greater consciousness, but there's also an aspect of consciousness that doesn't notice, but nevertheless is highly responsive. Your heart beats, you breathe, you grow your hair—you're doing all of it, but you don't know how it's done. In the same way that conscious attention is not aware of all the other operations of the body, you are not aware of your connection with the fundamental self. Leaves die and fall off the tree, and the next year there are more leaves and more fruit. You and I die and more babies are born. And if the whole human race dies, you bet your life there are creatures scattered throughout the multiplicity of galaxies who feel they are human. We might think these are different things, because we're unconscious of the intervals—we're not aware of the self with our conscious attention when our conscious attention isn't operating. But just as you don't notice what your pineal gland is doing right at this moment, you don't notice the connections that tie us all together—not only here and now, but forever and ever and ever.

We don't notice the self because the self doesn't need to look at itself. A knife doesn't need to cut itself, fire doesn't need to burn itself, water doesn't need to quench itself, and light doesn't need to shine on itself. However, the whole contention of Indian philosophy—especially Vedanta—is that it is possible in a certain way to become aware of yourself in this deepest sense and understand that you are the totality. In both Hindu and Buddhist philosophy, this is understood as moksha—liberation. Liberation from the hallucination that you are just some *poor little me*. It means to wake up from that kind of hypnosis and discover that you are something *being done* by this vast, incredible self that has no beginning, no end, neither continuation nor discontinuation—it's beyond all categorization whatsoever. As the Upanishads say, "It is not this, it is not that." Anything you can formulate, imagine, or picture will not be the self, so in order to know the self, you must get rid of every idea in your head. This doesn't mean to get rid of every sense impression and enter a catatonic state of total absorption. Full moksha is when you come back out of meditative absorption and see this everyday world just as it looks now, but you clearly see that it is all the self. You become aware of the tremendous interconnectedness of everything. You see that everything goes together, which is what we mean by relativity.

Relativity means relatedness—fronts go with backs, tops go with bottoms, insides with outsides, solids with spaces. Everything goes together. And it makes no difference if something lasts a long time or a short time—a galaxy goes together with all the universe just as much as a mosquito. From the standpoint of the self, time is completely relative. It's all a question of point of view or—to use a scientific expression—level of magnification. Look at what's in front of you with greater magnification and you'll see molecules, and look at those molecules with greater magnification, and you'll find space so vast between atoms that it's comparable to the distance between the sun and its planets. And it's the same thing with time. There could be vast universes full of empires and battleships and palaces and brothels and restaurants and orchestras—all in the tip of your fingernail. On the other hand, our whole world could be going on in the tip of somebody else's fingernail.

Human senses respond only to a very small band of the known spectrum of vibrations. But if our senses were in some way altered, we would see a rather different-looking world. There are an infinite number of possibilities of vibrations—worlds within worlds within worlds. However, having senses and noticing is fundamentally a selective process—it picks out particular vibrations from the larger array. When you play the piano, you don't take both hands and slam them down on the keys all at once—you select. Perception is a kind of piano playing. You pick out certain things as significant—that is to say, as constituting patterns. The whole universe seems to be a process of playing with different patterns. But no matter what pattern it plays—no matter what it does in whatever dimension or scale of time and space—it's all *on* the self.

There's a famous Zen koan: "Before your father and mother conceived you, what was your original nature?" That is, who were you before you were born into this life? It's the same sort of weird question as what it would be like to go to sleep and never wake up, or what was it like to wake up having not previously gone to sleep. It's very mysterious. And as you explore questions like these, you begin to feel that your existence is exceedingly odd. Odd because you are here and so easily might not have been. If your parents had never met, would you be here? If your parents met other people and had children, would one of those children be you? Of course it would. See, you can only be you by being someone, but every someone is you—every someone is *I*. Everybody feels that *I* in the same way. It's the same feeling, just as blue is the same color everywhere. That *I*-ness is the most fundamental thing in people and in the universe. Our *I* comes out of the central *I* like a single stem on a larger branch on an enormous tree, and this is why Hindu deities are shown with so many arms and faces. All arms are the arms of the divine; all faces are its masks.

In other words, there's really nothing to worry about. The important you is perfectly indestructible. Our comings and goings, fortunes and misfortunes, are all a sort of mirage. And the more we know about them, the more we know about the world, and the more diaphanous it seems—everything in the world has the characteristics of smoke. If you look at smoke through a sunbeam, it's full of whirls and designs and all kinds of marvelous things. And then it disappears. Everything is just like that.

There are two attitudes you can take about this state of affairs. On the one hand, you can see it all as lousy. You're given all of these feelings of love and attachment and joy, but eventually your teeth drop out, your eyes become feeble, you get cancer or cirrhosis of the liver or something like that, and it all falls apart. And it's too bad! So you decide not to get attached to things, you don't enjoy life, and you hold life at arm's length like a jilted lover. On the other hand, you can see the weaving of the smoke as incredibly beautiful, provided you don't try to lean on it. You can see it all as wonderful as long as you don't try to preserve it or catch hold of it. That's when you destroy it. In exactly the same way, there's really nothing in the way of form that you can lean on or grasp. And if you see that, then the world of forms is very beautiful—if you let it go.

When Hindu and Buddhist philosophers speak of detachment, it just means going with this whole thing and not resisting change. And if you do that, you can afford to go with it—you can afford to get mixed up in life and fall in love and get involved with all sorts of things. You can afford it *if* you know it's an illusion. This is where this word maya is crucial. Yes, maya means "illusion", but it also means magic, art, delineation, and measurement. Our English words *matter* and *material* are related to maya; but when we say "material" today, we think of something very real—not illusory at all. Well, measurement is certainly an illusion, because you don't find inches lying around—you can't pick up an inch. Inches and pounds and dollars and hours are actually imaginary, just like the self. The real self isn't material—it doesn't *matter*. That is, it doesn't exist for any purpose—it doesn't need to exist for any purpose. What purpose would it exist for? So the most important thing in the universe is the one thing that doesn't matter—the one thing that's totally and completely useless and that nobody can find.

A Zen master was once asked, "What is the most valuable thing in the world?" He replied, "The head of a dead cat." Why? Because no one can put a price on it. So the self—the Brahman—is like the head of a dead cat. But if you think that you need to go out and get a dead cat's head because there's something spiritual about it and it would be very good for you, you're putting the cart before the horse. And if you want to find the self because you'll be a better person or be better liked or be more constructive in society, that's trying to make the tail wag the dog. Knowing the self—Brahman—never does anybody any good if they're trying to make it do them any good. It's like when you relax and start to play and think, "This is good for me—it's exercise. It's also a break from work, and that's good—it will help me work better." Americans in particular are terrible at this. Everything you do is done for some serious reason—it's the Protestant conscience. But play is that which is done just for itself—for fun. And the self—atman, Brahman—exists for fun.

Work is something serious. It's what you do for a purpose, because you believe that you have to go on living. You have to work to survive, because you think you have to survive. But you don't have to. And this whole thing doesn't have to go on, which is why it does. I know that seems paradoxical, but think about it—life is full of examples of this. If I try to impress someone, I usually don't. If you try too hard with anything, you usually make a mess of it. So the one self behind the world is engaged in play, which is why it is said that Brahman does not actually *become* the world—Brahman *plays* at being the world, which is distinct from *working at it*.

But keep in mind that although I've used the words *one* and *central* to refer to the self, the Hindus don't use the same language other than poetically. The self is not one. Instead, the self is referred to as *nondual*. The opposite of one is many or none, so you can't call the self *one*, because that's an exclusive idea, and the self doesn't exclude anything. *Advaita*—nonduality—is meant to be a totally inclusive kind of unity. You can draw a three-dimensional object on a two-dimensional piece of paper, and a viewer will see the object in three dimensions because of one-pointed perspective, but it's an illusion. The third dimension can never be expressed on a flat surface. Similarly, *Advaita* is a word used specifically to designate what lies beyond all logical categories.

We are accustomed to use the word *play* in opposition to the word *work*, and so we regard play as something trivial and work as something serious. This shows up in our language: "You're only playing with me." But we also use the word in a nontrivial sense: "Have you heard Heifetz play the violin?" In that case, it refers to a high art form, but it's still play. When I do philosophy—like I'm doing now—I feel it is entertainment, but I hope it resembles listening to someone play beautiful music. I am not being serious, but I am being sincere. The difference between seriousness and sincerity is that seriousness is someone speaking in the context of the possibility of tragedy. Things might go absolutely wrong, so I put on a serious expression like a soldier on parade or someone in court or church. Everything is a matter of life and death. Which brings up the fundamental question: "Is God serious?" And—obviously—the answer is "No." And so the supreme self is quite useless. It doesn't matter, because it transcends all values of what is better or worse, what is up or down, what is good or bad. It weaves the world so that good and bad play together like the black and white pieces in a game of chess.

Children play with deep absorption and fascination. Mathematicians are entirely lacking in seriousness—they don't give a hoot in hell whether what they're doing has any practical application. They work on interesting puzzles and elegant and beautiful solutions to those puzzles. Musicians make series of interesting notes on instruments. What does any group of people like to do when they don't have to do anything? As far as I can tell, people get together and do something rhythmic—they dance, sing, and play games. Even in playing dice, there's a wonderful rhythm to shaking the cup and rolling the dice out on the table. Or dealing cards in poker. Or knitting. Or breathing. There are so many ways we love to experience rhythm. Our very existence is rhythm—waking, sleeping, eating, moving. And what's it all about? Does it really mean anything? Does it go anywhere? Fundamentally, the world is play.

When you examine vibration—particularly if you view vibration as a wave motion—you find a very peculiar thing: there's no such thing as half a wave. In nature, we never find crests without troughs or troughs without crests. No sound occurs unless there are beats and the intervals between them. This wave phenomenon is happening on ever so many scales—the fast wave of light, the slower waves of sound—and there are all sorts of other wave processes, such as the beat of the heart; the rhythm of breath, waking, sleeping; the movement of human life from birth to maturity to death. And the slower the wave goes, the more difficult it is to see that the crest and trough are inseparable, and this is how we become persuaded in the game of hide-and-seek. So we see the trough go down, down, down and think it keeps going forever—that it will never rise back up again into a crest. We forget that trough implies crest, and crest implies trough. There is no such thing as pure sound—sound is sound/silence. Light is light/darkness. Light is pulsation—between every light pulse there is the dark pulse.

This interplay can be seen in the way that Hindus calculate time—in units called *kalpas*, which are 4,320,000 years long. Now, don't take this too literally. It's meant to be symbolic or a rough guide, as opposed to some sort of divine revelation upon which one can make predictions and prophecies. For one whole kalpa, the world manifests, and in Sanskrit this is called a *manvantara*. This is when Brahman begins the hide-and-seek game by hiding—it hides in all of us and pretends it's us. Then that kalpa ends and another starts up—the *pralaya*. This is the period in which Brahman, as it were, comes out of the act and returns to itself in peace and bliss. This is a very logical idea. What would you do if you were God? As every child knows, the whole fun of things is to go on adventures, play make-believe, and create illusions—that is to say, patterns. Sometimes, in Hindu thought the world is represented as the dream of the godhead, and the godhead is illustrated as two-faced: one face is absorbed in the dream world and the other face is awake and liberated. In other words, from the viewpoint of the self—that is, the supreme self—the two kalpas I just described are simultaneous. But for human consumption, the pralaya and manvantara are represented in mythological form as occurring sequentially.

If you understand this point, you'll see that references to the *hereafter* are correctly understood as pointing to the *herein*—that is, a domain deeper than egocentric consciousness. When you get to the bottom of the egocentric consciousness, you get to its limit, which is figuratively its death. Then you go inward to the self, deeper than conscious attention, and in that way you go inward to eternity. You don't go *onward* to eternity. To go onward means time—more and more and more time in which things go round and round forever. But to go *in* is to go to eternity.

So we can speak metaphorically of the everlasting game of hide-and-seek in which the self plays with itself. It forgets who it is, then creeps up behind itself and says, "Boo!" And that's a great thrill. The self pretends that things are getting serious, just like a great actor on the stage. Even though the audience knows that what they see on stage is only a play, the actor's skill takes them in—they weep and laugh and sit on the edge of their seats with anticipation. They're utterly involved in what they really know is just a play. So that's what's going on here. Brahman is a tremendous actor with absolutely superb technique, so much so that Brahman takes itself in and feels that the play is real. We are all the Brahman acting out our own parts and playing the human game so beautifully that Brahman is enchanted, and this is what enchantment means—under the influence of a chant, hypnotized, spellbound, fascinated. And that fascination is maya.

Understanding that, let us consider the breakdown of a single kalpa, which consists of four *yugas*—yuga means an "epoch." The names of these eras—*krita* (sometimes called *satya*), *treta*, *dwapara*, and *kali*—are based on a Hindu game of dice in which there are four possible throws. The best throw is a four, which represents krita, the first era, which lasts 1,728,000 years. I never remember these numbers very well, so, again, don't take this too literally. The second-best throw is a three, which stands for treta—something like 1,296,000 years long. Then we have dwapara—864,000 years long—a dice throw of two. And, finally, one—the worst throw, kali. And that yuga lasts 432,000 years. Now, you see what's happening here. When manifestation first begins, everything is just glorious, because if you could dream anything you wanted to dream, you'd probably start with the most luscious dreams imaginable. But by the time you get to the treta yuga, something is a little wrong. Krita is foursquare—everything's perfect, and the square is an ancient symbol of perfection—but treta is a triangle. There's something missing; a little bit of uncertainty and danger enters the picture. And by the time we get to dwapara, the forces of light and darkness are equal—duality, the pair. But when we get to kali, the force of darkness overcomes everything.

Let's add these figures up, beginning with the "bad" side of all of this. Take one-third of the treta yuga, one-half of the dwapara yuga, and all of the kali yuga. When you add all that time up, you get the bad side taking up close to one-third of a kalpa. What's going on here? Well, it isn't a view of the cosmos in which good and evil are so evenly balanced that nothing happens. In this view, evil is just troublesome enough to give good a run for its money—you have to have some chaos in order to play the game of order against it. If order wins, there's no more game; if chaos wins, there's no further game; if they're equally balanced, it's a stalemate. So here's what happens: chaos is always losing, but is never defeated. It's a good loser. And that's a game worth the candle. In chess, if you play an opponent who can always defeat you, you'll soon stop playing with them, just as you'll stop playing with someone you can beat all of the time. But if there remains a certain uncertainty of outcome, and you win some of the time, then it's a good game.

Again, all this is simply numerical symbolism. The mythology states that we are now in the kali yuga, which began a little before 3000 BCE, so we have a long way to go before this thing ends—if you insist on taking this literally. Of course, people have been talking about the world being in the kali yuga for some time. There are Egyptian inscriptions from 6000 BCE or so that describe the world as going hopelessly to the dogs. It seems this has always been the complaint.

There's another important thing to consider about this mythology. Brahman is represented in three aspects—Brahma, the creating principle; Vishnu, the preserving principle; and Shiva, the destroying principle. Shiva—who is always represented in Hindu imagery as a yogi—is very important here. He is the destroyer in the sense that he liberates—he cracks the shells of eggs so that chickens can come forth, for example. Shiva also opens up mothers so that their children can be born. He's also found in deliberate acts of destruction such as bonfires, which is why devotees of Shiva like to meditate along the banks of the Ganges where dead bodies are burned, because through destruction, life is constantly renewed. And Shiva's paramour is named Kali, who is much worse than Shiva. Kali has black skin and is extremely beautiful, but she has a long tongue, and her eyeteeth are like fangs. In her right hand, she holds a scimitar, and in her left hand, she carries a severed head by its hair. So Kali is what most people dread—she's the awful awfuls. She's outer darkness, the end, the principle of total night, and she's sometimes represented as a bloodsucking octopus or a female spider who eats its spouse.

But there are those in India—Sri Ramakrishna, for example—who see Kali as the supreme mother goddess. For them, Kali has two faces: playful and terrifying, loving and devouring, savior and destroyer. In this way, meditating on Kali will help one see the light principle in the very depths of darkness, and you can do this personally by going to the aquarium and studying the monsters of the deep that make you feel most uncomfortable. Meditating in this way is like putting manure on soil—out of all this apparently morbid and dismal thinking, bright things arise. And devotees realize that Kali is the most far-out act that the supreme self can put on—the symbol of complete alienation from itself. Just like children sitting around having a competition as to who can make the most hideous face, things get worse and worse as time goes on until the end of the kali yuga when Shiva puts on a black appearance with ten arms and dances a dance called the *tandava*, in which the whole universe is destroyed in fire. And when Shiva turns around to leave the stage, you see the face of Brahma—the Creator—on the back of his head. And the whole thing starts again.

So this involves certain ideas that are quite alien to the West. To begin with, the idea of the world as play. Our Lord God in the West tends to be overserious, and none of the famous Christian artists ever painted Christ laughing or smiling. He's always this tragic figure who has this sort of look in his eye that says, "One of these days, you and I have to get together for a very serious talk." And then there's the notion of cyclic time. Most of us live in linear time, which goes back to the influence of Saint Augustine and his interpretation of the Bible. For a while, it was in fashion in modern scholarship to say that Judaism gave us the idea of history, but Hindus have no interest in history whatsoever—or not until recent times, at least—to the total exasperation of historians. There is no way of finding textual evidence of the age of most Hindu scriptures, because they are only interested in human events as archetypal occurrences—as repetitions of great mythological themes. So if a document begins with a certain adventure that happens to King So-and-So—whom everybody knew at the time—in the next generation they change the name of the past king to the name of the current king, because the story was typical anyway, and they just wanted to use the name of a king everybody knows.

On the other hand, according to our scholars, the Jews were historically minded because they remembered the story of their descent from Adam and Abraham, the great event of the liberation from Egypt, and the triumphant reign of King David. Then things go sliding downhill as other political forces become stronger and stronger, and so the people get fixed on the idea that one day is going to be the day of the Lord, and the Messiah will come and put an end to history and there will be the restoration of paradise. See, this is linear. There isn't the idea of the world having been created many times before and coming to an end many times before, too. There's a clear ascent from start to finish, from alpha to omega. And when Saint Augustine was thinking about this, he realized that cyclic time wouldn't work for Christianity—it would mean that Jesus would have to be crucified for the salvation of the world over and over again. What they call the *one, full, perfect, sufficient sacrifice, oblation, and satisfaction for the sins of the whole world* could not be so. So, once is enough.

Of course, Augustine got his hierarchies confused. It's true that there is one sacrifice, but it's on the plane of eternity. On the plane of time, eternal things can repeat again and again. But that's how we were handed down linear time, so we're always thinking of a progression that will take us steadily and faster into an increasingly perfect world. I think this shows a rather naïve view of human nature.

Humans tend to smash what they create and say, "Let's do it all over again." So I don't think it's too realistic to think that human beings will get better and better and better, because they'll soon get tired of it all and decide to be as awful as possible. There was certainly that element in Nazism—how awful can you get? How brutal? How destructive? Within all of us, there is an element represented by Shiva Kali—it's always there. So Hindus look at the world with a hardboiled realism this way, seeing both terror and magnificence, love and fury, as two faces of the same thing. You might look at this and wonder if any peace is possible, because these cycles go on and on and on without end. Even Hindus sometimes wonder if Brahman ever gets tired of it all, but Brahman doesn't, because you only get tired of things you remember. Brahman doesn't have to remember anything, because for the self there is no time—there's only an eternal now.

The secret to waking up from the drama—all these endless cycles—is to realize that only the present exists. It's the only time there is. And when you become awake to that, boredom ends, and you are delivered from the cycles—not in the sense that they disappear, but that you no longer go through them. Well, you *do* go through them, but you realize they're not going anywhere. And you don't even try to hurry up and get to the end of it all faster, because just like music, the point of listening isn't to get to the end of the piece—you can sit back with interest and let it all be. You can look at every little detail of life in a new way, saying, "Oh! Look at that!" By living totally here and now, one's eyes are opened in astonishment.

14

Insiders and Outsiders

The self is not something into which we come, but out of which we proceed. We say, "I came into this world," as if we came from somewhere else altogether, from someplace outside, but we don't. We come out of this world, in the same way as leaves come out of a tree. We are an expression of the world and an expression of the self—the basis, the ground of all that fundamentally is. So I want to discuss the human world as the self.

In the known history of humans, there have been three types of cultures—I'll call them hunting, agrarian, and industrial. Hunting cultures came first, and agrarian cultures arose when hunters settled in certain areas and learned to farm, which led to established communities. And when a culture shifts like this from hunting to an agrarian way of life, two very important changes occur. First, in a hunting culture, everyone is an expert in the whole culture—they spend a good deal of time alone in forests and hills and plains, so they must know how to make clothes, how to cook, how to build structures, how to fight, how to ride, and all sorts of things. But when people settle in communities, they begin to divide up the labor, because it's more practical when living together that certain people specialize in some tasks and other people specialize in others.

Second, hunting cultures and agrarian cultures differ greatly when it comes to religion. In a hunting culture, the primary religious figure is the shaman, and the shaman is a weird individual. I don't mean weird as in strange or queer, but more in an ancient sense of the word that indicates a sense of magic. A shaman is someone with a peculiar type of sensitivity who becomes initiated into shamanism by going off by themselves for a long time into the depths of the forest or the heights of the mountains. In that isolation, they encounter a domain of consciousness that we call all sorts of names—the spirit world, the ancestors, the gods, whatever. And the shaman's knowledge of that world gives them peculiar powers of healing, prophecy, and magic. The main thing to note about shamans is that their initiation comes from themselves. In other words, they are not given their power or authority from any religious order or guru. On the other hand, the religious figure of the agrarian community is a priest. And a priest invariably receives their power from a community of priests or a particular guru—in other words, from tradition. Tradition is all-important in the agrarian community.

Reasonably enough, the first communities were stockade enclosures. They were made of palings, which is why we speak of people being within or beyond the pale. These primitive, stockaded communities were often settled at crossroads for obvious reasons—that's where roads cross and people meet. So these communities were liable to have four gates with crossing main streets that immediately establish four divisions of the city. Oddly enough, in Hindu society there are four castes based on the four fundamental divisions of labor—the caste of priests, the Brahmana; the caste of rulers and warriors, the Kshatriya; the caste of merchants and traders, the Vaishya; and the laborers, the Sudra. These are the four principle roles in the world of settled humanity.

When you enter society, you are born into one of these castes, which is understandable in a community without a generalized system of education that invites you to consider the idea that you might become anything. In a society of castes, if you grow up as a carpenter's son, it never occurs to you to do anything else but carpentry—why would you? You might become a *better* carpenter than your father, but that's about it, because this sort of life is natural to you—you don't find it particularly objectionable. Of course—as happened in India—over time this type of society develops all sorts of complications and rituals and prohibitions that make the system rigid and unjust and cumbersome.

That aside, when you grow up in this type of society, you go through an evolution in your development within your caste. You begin as a student or apprentice—a *brahmacharya*—and then you eventually become a householder, the stage of *grihastha*. A householder has two duties: *artha*, duties of citizenship like partaking in the political life of the community, and *kama*, cultivating the senses of aesthetic and sensual beauty—the arts of love, beautification, dress, cooking, and that sort of thing. So, the *Kama Sutra* is the scripture about love—the great Hindu manual on the sexual arts. Every child should read the *Kama Sutra* upon reaching puberty so they will get some sense of how to make love without acting like a mere baboon. Then there is the *Arthashastra*, which is the scripture for the Kshatriya caste. But for all the castes, beyond the stage of householder, there's also one's duty of *dharma*, and this word has multiple meanings in Sanskrit—law, justice, rightness, method. So when we speak of the Buddhadharma—the Buddha's doctrine—the word means "method," not "law." In any case, a citizen in this sort of society has to conform to dharma, which is to say the ritual, ethical, and moral game rules for the community.

Now, when a person goes through these stages and performs these duties, and the eldest child has assumed governorship of the household, the father or mother may now enter into a new stage of life altogether—the *vanaprastha*, which means "forest dweller." See what has happened? We came out of the forest as a hunter, settled in the community, and indulged in the social games of the world that are everybody's dharma or duty. In ancient times, once you fulfilled these duties, you actually did go out into the forest and became—of all things—a *sramana*, which is thought to be related to the word *shaman*. So the individual played the world's game, then went off by themselves to find out who they really were.

You have a role conception—a mask conception—of yourself, because other people tell you who you are. In every social interchange, we are constantly telling other people who they are in our most common remarks. Everything leads up to that. The way I act toward you and the way you act toward me tell me who I am and who you are. You read these words or listen to me talk, so I become some kind of teacher, and you tell yourself that you are some kind of student. At work or at home or in between, everybody around you is telling you who you are by expecting certain behaviors from you, and if you're a reasonable and socially inclined person, you perform these behaviors, because that's what's expected of you.

So the sramana or vanaprastha first practices *mauna*—a vow of silence that might last months or years. After about a month of this, you stop thinking in words, and that's very curious. You stop classifying and codifying the world by thinking, so all your senses take on a tremendous intensity—sunsets appear incredibly more vivid, and flowers are more enchanting. And at this point, the new vanaprastha will seek out a guide or guru who has been through the whole discipline of yoga, because the new retreatant can lose all moral discrimination and get into trouble. That's why it's said that when a guru accepts a student, the guru becomes responsible for that individual's karma, which means "activity" but also "results of activity." And the new vanaprastha removes every sign that would identify them as a particular someone—they abandon their name, they put on some kind of yellow robe or wear a loin cloth or go naked, and they often cover themselves with ashes, and their hair gets matted. They don't take care of themselves anymore in that way, because they're now outside the pale.

So, you have here a marvelous microcosm—a political and social analogue of the manifestation and withdrawal of the worlds, of the self playing the game of being all of us and then—as each individual reaches moksha—the self realizes that it is the self. And there are four castes, just as there are four yugas to the kalpa cycle. And the outgoing state of the vanaprastha is a higher evolutionary state than a person in a hunting culture, who is primitive. The vanaprastha isn't simply going back to where they came from—they have spiraled to an equivalent position, but at a higher level. What they have gained in the interim is self-awareness. See, it's not fun to be happy and not know it—we need a certain resonance. Self-consciousness is an echo in our heads—an echo of what we do but wouldn't be aware of doing if there weren't an echo. So self-consciousness is neurological resonance.

However, resonance can get troublesome if it's not properly worked out. You can get echoes that won't stop. You go into a great cave somewhere and shout, "Hi!" and it just keeps repeating "hi" forever off in the distance. That's very confusing. It's the sort of snarl that self-consciousness can get into, and we call this anxiety. When I keep thinking over and over again, "Did I do the right thing?"—if I'm constantly aware of myself in a kind of anxious, critical way—my resonance becomes too high, and I get confused and jittery. But if you learn that self-consciousness has limits, that self-awareness cannot possibly enable you to be free of making mistakes, you can learn to be spontaneous in spite of being self-aware. And you can enjoy the echo.

So after developing self-consciousness through the course of their lives, vanaprasthas become again as children. They get what Freud said a child has at the beginning—an "oceanic feeling" of being one with the universe. The vanaprastha gets that back. However, it's not a child's oceanic feeling—it's an adult's oceanic feeling. The psychoanalysts don't discuss this, because according to them all oceanic feelings are regressive. But a mature oceanic feeling is as different from an immature oceanic feeling as an oak is different from an acorn. And you can have this sensation of total unity with the cosmos without forgetting society's game rules with regard to you. In other words, it doesn't mean that you forget your address, phone number, and given name—you remember all that, *and* you play the game when necessary, but you always know that it's a game.

So, how can an individual realize that they are the universal self? In what way can a person who is under the impression that they are a separate individual enclosed in a bag of skin effectively realize that they are Brahman? This, of course, is a curious question. It proposes a journey to the place where you already are. Now, it's true that you may not know that you are there, but you are. And if you take a journey to the place where you are, you will visit many places other than the place where you are, and perhaps you find, through some long experience, that all the places you go to are not the place you wanted to find. It may occur to you that you were already there in the beginning. And that is the dharma, or "method," as I prefer to translate the word. That's the method that all gurus and spiritual teachers fundamentally use. So, they are all tricksters.

Why use *trickster* as a word to describe them? Did you know that it's terribly difficult to surprise yourself on purpose? Somebody else has to do it for you, which is why a guru or teacher is so often necessary. And there are many kinds of gurus; but among human gurus, there are square gurus and beat gurus. Square gurus take you through the regular channels; beat gurus lead you in by means that are very strange indeed—they are rascals. Also, friends can act as gurus. And then there are gurus who aren't people, like situations or books. Regardless, the guru's job is to show the inquirer in some effective way that they are already what they are looking for.

In Hindu traditions, realizing who you really are is called *sadhana*, which means "discipline." Sadhana is the way of life that is necessary to follow in order to escape from the illusion that you are merely a skin-encapsulated ego. Sadhana comprises yoga, which has the Sanskrit root *yuj*, which means "to join," and it is from this root that we have the English words *yoke*, *junction*, and *union*. Strictly speaking, yoga means "the state of union"—the state in which the individual self, the *jivatman*, finds that it is ultimately atman. So a yogi is someone who has realized that union. But normally, *yoga* as a word isn't used that way; it's normally used to describe a practice of meditation whereby one comes into the state of union, and in that sense, a yogi is a traveler or seeker who is on the way to that union. Of course, strictly speaking, there is no method to arrive at the place where you already are. No amount of searching will uncover the self, because all searching implies the absence of the self—the big self, the Self with a capital *S*. So to seek it is to thrust it away. And to practice a discipline to attain it is to postpone realization.

There's a famous Zen story of a monk sitting in meditation. The master comes along and asks, "What are you doing?" And the monk replies, "Oh, I'm meditating so I can become a Buddha." Well, the master sits down nearby, picks up a brick, and starts rubbing it. And the monk asks, "What are you doing?" The master says, "Oh, I'm rubbing this brick to make it into a mirror." And the monk says, "No amount of rubbing a brick can turn it into a mirror." To which the master replies, "And no amount of zazen will turn you into a Buddha." They don't like this story very much in modern-day Japan.

Suppose I were to tell you that you, right now, are the great Self—the Brahman. Now, you might feel somewhat intellectually sympathetic to this idea, but you don't really feel it. You're looking for a way to feel it—a practice for getting there. But you don't *really* want to feel it; you're frightened of it. So you get this or that practice so you can put it off, so you can feel that you have a long way to go, and maybe after you've suffered enough, *then* you can realize you are the atman. Why put it off? Because we are brought up in a social scheme that tells us we have to deserve what we get, and the price to pay for all good things is suffering. But all that is mere postponement. We are afraid here and now to see the truth. And if we had the nerve—you know, real nerve—we'd see it right away. But that's when we immediately feel that we shouldn't have nerve like that, because it would be awful. After all, we're supposed to feel like a poor little me who has to work and work and suffer in order to become something far away and great, like a Buddha or *jivanmukta*—someone who becomes liberated.

So you can suffer for it. There are all kinds of ways invented for you to do this. You can discipline yourself and gain control of your mind and do all sorts of extraordinary things—like drink water in through your rectum and push a peanut up a mountain with your nose. There are all sorts of accomplishments you can engage in. But they have absolutely nothing to do with the realization of the self.

The realization of the self fundamentally depends on coming off it, just as when someone is putting on some kind of act, and we say, "Oh, come off it." And some people can come off it—they laugh, because they suddenly realize they've been making a fool of themselves.

So that's the job of the trickster—the guru, the teacher—to help you come off it. And to this end, the guru will come up with all sorts of exercises to get you to come off it. And maybe after you get enough discipline and frustration and suffering, you'll finally give it all up and realize that you were there from the beginning, and there was nothing to realize in the first place. See, the guru is very clever. They don't go out on the streets and preach and tell you that you need to be converted—they sit down under a tree and wait. And people start coming around and bringing their problems and propositions to the guru, and the guru answers and challenges them in whatever way they think is appropriate to their situation. Now, if you've got a thin shell, and your mask is easily dispatched with, the guru uses the easy method. They'll say, "Come off it, Shiva! Stop pretending you're this guy here. I know who you are!" But most people won't respond to that. Most people have very thick shells, so the guru has to invent ways of cracking those shells.

To understand yoga, you should read Patanjali's Yoga Sutra. There are so many translations, and I'm not sure which is the best. This sutra begins, "Now yoga is explained." That's the first verse, and the commentators say that "now" in this context carries the meaning that you're supposed to know other material beforehand. Specifically, you're supposed to be a civilized human being before you begin yoga—you're supposed to have been disciplined in artha, kama, and dharma. You're supposed to have engaged in politics, the arts of sensuality, and justice before you can begin yoga. The next verse is *"Yogash chitta vritti nirodha,"* ("Yoga is the cessation of revolutions of the mind,") and this can mean many things—stop the waves of the mind, attain a perfectly calm mind, stop thinking entirely, or even eliminate all content from the mind. How can you do that? Well, the sutra goes on to give you particular steps: *pranayama, pratyahara, dharana, dhyana,* and *samadhi.*

Pranayama means controlling the breath; pratyahara refers to preliminary concentration; dharana is a more intense form of concentration; dhyana—the same dhyana from which the word Zen comes—means profound union between subject and object; and then there's samadhi—the attainment of nondualistic consciousness. See what's happening here? First, you learn to control your breath. And breathing is a very strange thing, because breathing can be viewed both as a voluntary *and* involuntary action. You can feel that you breathe, yet you can also feel that breathing breathes you. And in yoga, there are all sorts of fancy ways to breathe that are very amusing to practice, because you can get quite high on them. So this sutra sets you up with all sorts of tricks, and if you are bright, you may begin to realize some things at this point.

But if you are not very bright, you'll have to go on to work on concentration. You learn to concentrate the mind on one point. Now, this can be an absolutely fascinating undertaking. Here's one way to try it out: find some bright, polished surface—say, on copper or glass or something—and select on it some reflection of light. Now, look at it and put your eyes out of focus so that the bright spot appears to be fuzzy, like a fuzzy circle. You'll see a definite pattern of blur, and you'll have a wonderful time looking at that. Then get your eyes back into focus and look at an intense light and go deep into it, like falling down a funnel, and at the end of the funnel is this intense light. Just go in and in and in—it's a most thrilling experience.

So you're doing this kind of practice when the guru suddenly wakes you up. And they say, "What are you looking at that light for?" And you stammer something about wanting realization because we live in a world in which we identify ourselves with the ego, and we therefore get into trouble and suffer. And the guru asks, "Well, are you afraid of that?" And you respond, "Yes." Well, then the guru points out to you that all you're doing is practicing yoga out of fear—you're just escaping and running away. And how far do you think you can get into realization through fear? So then you think, "Well, now I've got to practice yoga, but not with a fearful motive."

And all the while, the guru is watching you. They're a highly sensitive person, and they know exactly what you're doing—they know exactly what your motive is. So they put you on to the kick of getting a pure motive, which means getting a very deep control of your emotions. So you try not to have impure thoughts. You try and try and maybe manage to repress as many impure thoughts as possible, and then one day the guru asks, "Why are you repressing your thoughts? What's your motive here?" And then you find out that you had an impure motive for trying to have a pure mind. You did it for the same old reason. From the very beginning, you were afraid, because you wanted to play one up on the universe.

Eventually, you see how crazy your mind is. It can only go in circles. Everything your mind does to get out of the trap puts it more securely in the trap. Every step toward liberation ties you up even more. You started with molasses in one hand and feathers in the other, and the guru made you clap your hands together and then told you to pick the feathers off. And the more you try to do so, the more mess you make. Meanwhile, as you get more and more involved in this curious process, the guru tells you how you're progressing. "You attained the eighth stage today. Congratulations. Now you only have fifty-six steps remaining." And when you get to that sixty-fourth stage, the guru knows how to spin it and drag it all out, because you are ever so hopeful that you'll get that thing, just as you might win a prize or win a special job or great distinction and finally *be* somebody. That was your motivation all along, only it's very spiritual here. It's not for worldly recognition, but you want to be recognized by the gods and angels—it's the same story on a higher level.

So the guru keeps holding out all these baits, and the student keeps taking the bait. And the guru holds out more baits until the student gets the realization that they're just running around faster and faster in a squirrel cage. I mean, the student is making an enormous amount of progress, but they're not getting anywhere. And this is how the guru tricks you. The guru impresses this realization upon you by these methods until you finally find out that you—as an ego, as what you ordinarily call your mind—are a mess. And you just can't do this thing. You can't do it by any of the means that have been presented to you. You can now concentrate, yes, but you discover you've been concentrating for the wrong reason, and there's no way of doing it for the right reason.

Krishnamurti did this to people. He was a very clever guru. And early twentieth-century mystic G.I. Gurdjieff, too, although he played the same game in a different way. He made his students watch themselves constantly, and told them to never, never be absentminded. And the Japanese sword teachers do the same thing. Their first lesson is to always be alert—constantly—because you never know where or when the attack is going to come. Now, do you know what happens when you try to always be on the alert? You *think* about being alert—you're not alert. And you're a hopeless prey to the enemy. So the trick is to be simply awake and relaxed. Then all your nerve ends are working and whenever the attack comes, you're ready. The great teachers liken this to a barrel of water—the water sits there in the barrel, and as soon as you put a hole in the barrel, the water just falls out. It doesn't have to think about it. In the same way, when the mind is in a proper state, it is ready to respond in any direction without any sense of being taut or anxious. And the minute anything happens, it's right there, because it didn't have to overcome anything, like coming back from the opposite direction to respond to an attack. See, if you're set for the attack to come from over there, and it comes from here, you have to pull back from there and come here, but by then, it's too late. So sit in the middle and don't expect the attack to come from any particular direction.

In yoga, you can be watchful and concentrated and alert, but all that will ever teach you is what not to do—how *not* to use the mind. You have to just let it happen, like going to sleep. You can't *try* to go to sleep. It's the same with digesting your food—you can't try to digest your food. And it's the same with liberation—you have to let yourself wake up. When you find out there isn't any way of forcing it, maybe you'll stop forcing it. But most people don't believe this. They say, "Well, that won't work for me. I'm very unevolved. I'm just poor little me and if I don't force it, nothing will happen." I know some people who think they have to struggle and strain to have a bowel movement—they think they have to work to make it happen. But all this is based on a lack of faith—not trusting life. How do you get people to trust life? You have to trick them. They won't jump into the water, so you have to throw them in. And if they're very unwilling to be thrown in, they're going to take diving lessons or read books about diving or do preliminary exercises or stand at the edge of the diving board and inquire which is the right posture until somebody comes up from behind and kicks them in the butt to get them in the water.

And there's the most amazing gamesmanship that goes on in the whole domain of yoga and spiritual practice. You will be astounded. One of the games is to find a little flaw in you, which truly works, because everybody has a place inside where they can be jiggled a bit—something they're ashamed of. And we sometimes think that others can see this—that somewhere deep down, we're the awful awfuls. This plays out in religious competition. Let's say you've had years of therapy, and you meet with some Catholics. They'll say something like, "Well, all that therapy is fine, of course, but it's not nearly enough." Or you're a Catholic, and you go to some Buddhist outfit. They'll say, "Yes, Catholicism teaches some basic virtues, but it doesn't go anywhere near the heart of things, and it doesn't have an elaborate system of meditation like we have." Or you're a Buddhist, and you visit a Hindu group. They'll say, "Buddhism is great up to a certain point. They can attain a very high stage of realization, but there's something a lot higher than that they just don't get." And you'll find this all over the world—everybody claiming to have that little extra essence that others don't have.

What's going on here? Are they all frauds? Are they all just out to get you into their society? Sometimes yes. But other times, they're just trying to see whether you'll fall for it—they're testing you out. This is called *upaya*—"skillful method." And if you fall for the promise of that little extra special thing that's supposed to be right around the corner, then they've got you. Or rather, you've got yourself in the mix, and you have to work at this and work at that and so on until you find out that you were being made a monkey of. And you were being made a monkey of because you *could* be made a monkey of. You hadn't yet arrived. You didn't yet have the nerve to be you—to be the self. You always had to feel that there was something beyond, something else, something higher or better. That's why groups like the Masons have such success. They have thirty-three degrees, and you can climb that ladder your whole life—the more degrees the merrier. Some groups have hundreds of degrees, and they're an immense success because you can just keep postponing your liberation indefinitely. But when you get it, it happens instantly. And it happens instantly whether you put in thirty years of practice or whether you put in three minutes—it's the same liberation.

Let's go back to the vanaprastha—the person in Hindu society who has played the social game their entire life and now devotes themselves to self-discovery. This was actually something allowed more freely in medieval Western society, which revered and encouraged hermits, monks, and nuns of various types. In India, you couldn't join a different caste, but it was easier in European society—all you had to do was become literate (*cleric* simply means a "literate person"). You could be born as a serf, join a monastery, become literate, become a priest, or even an archbishop. It was the only way to cross castes, and through literacy, our caste system eventually began to break down, because we got the idea of choosing one's own vocation—that is, not simply following what one's parents did.

But checking out of the typical social game is not encouraged in contemporary society. The Catholic Church and some other religious institutions support hermits and monastics, but they're in the great minority. And you can't just check out of the game on your own without tremendous difficulty. If you do, you're seen as a deadbeat and a poor consumer. Some people drop out of college because they think it's stupid—maybe we call them beatniks—but the city doesn't like it very much. See, these dropouts don't own the right sort of cars, so the local car salesman isn't doing business through them; and they don't have lawns, so nobody can sell them lawnmowers; and they don't really use dishwashers or other appliances, because they don't really need them. And they wear blue jeans and things like that, so the local clothing stores feel a bit put out by having these people around who have very little and live very simply. Well, you can't have that. Everybody must live in a complicated way—you've got to have the right kind of car that identifies you as a person of substance and status and all that.

Why is this a problem? There's always an inconsiderable minority of people in society who are nonjoiners, but insecure societies are the most intolerant of those who check out of the game. These societies are so unsure of the validity of their game rules that they demand that everyone play the game. Now, that's a double blind. You can't tell a person that they *must* play, because then you're requiring them to do something that will be acceptable only if they do it voluntarily. So "everyone must play" is a rule in the United States, and it's a rule in most democratic governments because they are very uneasy—everyone is responsible, at least theoretically. Now, that's terrifying. If anyone can supposedly do whatever they want or think whatever they think, it means we're all unsettled. Therefore, we have to become more and more conformist. Rugged individualism always leads to conformism. People get scared, they herd together, they wear the same clothes, and the clothes just get duller and drabber.

Democracy as we have tried it started out on the wrong foot. We took the Christian scriptures that say that everybody is equal in the sight of God and made it to mean that everybody is *inferior* in the sight of God. And this is a parody of mysticism. Because originally, mysticism meant that, from the standpoint of God, all people are divine, which is a far different thing. So this is why all bureaucracies are rude, why police are rude, why you are made to wait in lines for everything, and why everyone is treated as some kind of crook. And a society like this, that views everybody as inferior, turns quickly into fascism because of its terror of the outsider.

A free and easy society loves outsiders. It knows that the outsider is doing for us what we haven't got the guts to do for ourselves.

The outsider lives up there in the mountains at the highest peak of human evolution—their consciousness is one with the divine, and that's just great. It makes you feel a little better to have somebody like that around. That person is realized—they know what it's all about. So we need those people, even if they aren't playing our game, because it reminds the government in no uncertain terms that there's something more important going on. That's why wise kings keep court fools—the fool reminds the king that he's going to die, that he's mortal. The fool lets the king know that there are forces and domains way, way beyond that of the king's. But that's very difficult for a democracy to realize, because it's insecure. That's why in our present world, it's nearly impossible to abandon your nationality. As Henry David Thoreau put it, "Wherever you may seek solitude, men will ferret you out and compel you to belong to their desperate company of odd fellows."

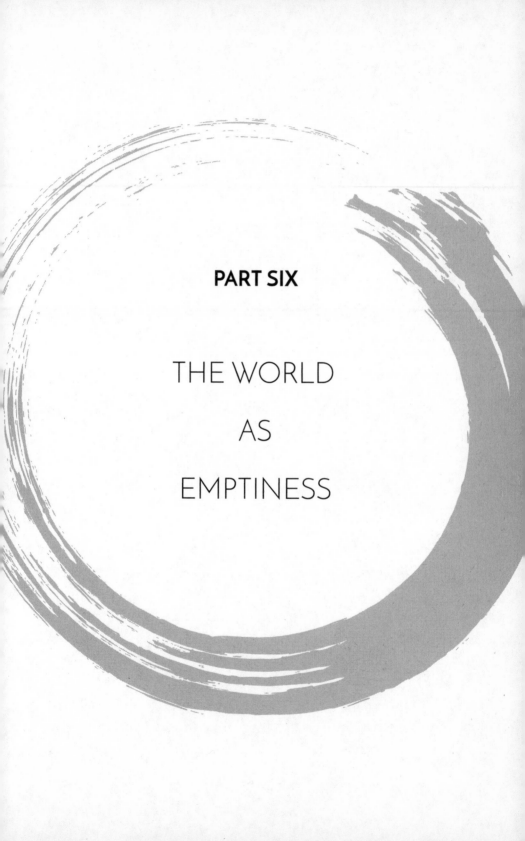

PART SIX

THE WORLD

AS

EMPTINESS

15

The Buddhist Method

There's a sense that Buddhism is Hinduism stripped for export. Hinduism isn't just a religion, it's a whole culture—a social and legal system that includes everything from etiquette to housing, food, and art. Hindus don't make a division between religion and everything else—religion is not a department of life. And when religion and culture are inseparable, it's very difficult to export the cultural aspect, because it conflicts with established traditions, manners, and customs of other people. So what essentials of Hinduism could be exported? When you answer this question approximately, you get Buddhism.

The essence of Hinduism isn't doctrine or discipline, it's moksha—liberation. You discover that you are on one level an illusion, but on another level, you are what's called the self—the one self that is all there is. And the universe is the game of the self that plays hide-and-seek forever and ever. When it hides, it hides so well that it pretends to be all of us and all things whatsoever, and we don't know this because the self is playing *hide*. But when it plays *seek*, it enters onto a path of yoga, and by following this path, it wakes up, and the veils fall from its eyes.

Similarly, the only really important thing about Buddhism is the experience of awakening. *Buddha* is a title, not a name. It comes from the Sanskrit root *bud* that sometimes means "to know," but a better meaning is "to wake." From this root, you get *bodhi*—the state of being awakened—so Buddha means "the awakened one." And the person called *the* Buddha is only one of myriads, because the Buddhists are quite sure that our world is only one among billions, and that Buddhas come and go in all the worlds. However, every so often there comes into the world what you might call a big Buddha—a very important Buddha. So the historic Buddha in our world—Gautama—was one of these big Buddhas. It's said he was the son of a prince who ruled part of Nepal around 600 BCE. Most of you will know the story of his life, but the point is that when in ancient India a man was called a Buddha—or *the* Buddha—it was a title of a very exalted nature. And a Buddha is considered superior to all gods and angels, because exalted beings such as these are still in the wheel of becoming—still in the chains of karma. These beings are still going round the wheel from life after life after life because they still thirst for existence—or, to put it in Hindu terms, the self is still playing the game of not being itself.

Here is the Buddha's experience of awakening: After seven years of extreme asceticism—fasting, lying on beds of nails, sleeping on broken rocks, and so on—after doing all of these various practices to break down egocentricity, to become detached, and to exterminate his desire for life, he found it all to be futile. One day, Gautama broke his discipline and accepted a bowl of milk from a girl who was looking after cattle. And suddenly—in tremendous relaxation—he went and sat down under a tree to see that everything he had been doing was on the wrong track. You can't make a silk purse out of a sow's ear. And no amount of effort will make a person who believes themselves to be an ego become truly unselfish. As long as you think and feel that you are contained in a bag of skin and that's all, there's no way whatsoever for you to behave unselfishly.

Well, you can imitate unselfishness. You can go through all sorts of highly refined forms of unselfishness, but you are still tied to the wheel of becoming by the golden chains of your good deeds, just as obviously bad people are tied to it by the iron chains of their misbehaviors.

This manifests in many ways—from spiritually proud people who believe they possess the one true teaching, to those who claim they are the most tolerant and inclusive and accepting, which is only a game called *being more tolerant and inclusive and accepting than everybody else*. The egocentric being is always in its own trap.

The Buddha saw that all his yoga exercises and ascetic disciplines had just been a way of trying to get himself out of the trap in order to save his own skin, in order to find peace for himself. Well, he realized that this is an impossible thing to do, because the motivation behind everything ruins the project. The Buddha found out that there was no trap to get out of except himself—trap and trapped are one. And when you understand that, there isn't any trap left. So as a result of this experience, he formulated what he called the dharma—his method. And it's absolutely important to remember that the method of Buddhism is dialectic. That is, the Buddha didn't teach a doctrine in the sense that Christianity or Judaism or Islam do. All of Buddhism is a discourse, and what most people suppose are its foundational teachings are only the opening stages of the dialogue.

Now, the Buddha formulated his teachings to be very easy to remember—all Buddhist scriptures are full of mnemonic tricks. Things are numbered in ways that are easy to remember. So the Buddha proposed the Four Noble Truths: *dukkha, trishna, nirvana,* and *marga*. His main concern was the first one—dukkha—which means "suffering, pain, frustration, and chronic dis-ease." It's the opposite of *sukha*, which refers to happiness, bliss, pleasure, and so on. So the problem of dukkha is that we suffer, we don't want to suffer, and we want to find someone or something that can solve the problem. And so the Buddha pointed out that there isn't anything in the world—in the material, psychic, or spiritual world—that you can hold on to for safety. Nothing. And not only is there nothing to hang on to, there is no *you* to hang on with—that's the teaching of *anatman*, or no self. In other words, all clinging to life is an illusory hand grasping at smoke. And if you get that into your head and see that it is so, nobody has to tell you that you ought not to grasp. See, Buddhism is not essentially moralistic.

The moralists tell people they ought to be unselfish when they still feel like egos, so the moralists' efforts are always and invariably futile. All they're doing is sweeping dust under the carpet.

The second of the Four Noble Truths regards the cause of suffering, which is trishna. It's related to the English word *thirst*, and it's often translated as desire, craving, clinging, grasping, or—to use a modern term of psychology—blocking. For example, when somebody is blocked, and they dither and hesitate and don't know what to do, they are—in the strictest Buddhist sense—*attached*. They're stuck. But a Buddha doesn't get stuck—they cannot be fazed. Just like water, a Buddha always flows, and even if you try to stop water by damming it up, it just gets higher and higher until it overflows the dam. Well, the Buddha said that dukkha comes from trishna—we suffer because we cling to the world. And we cling to the world because we don't realize that the world is *anitya*—that is, impermanent—and anatman. So try not to grasp.

But this poses a problem. A student who has begun this dialogue with the Buddha will make various efforts to give up desire, and this student will rapidly discover that they are desiring not to desire. And when the student takes this problem back to the teacher, the teacher will say, "Well, just try to give up desiring as much as you can. Don't go beyond the point of which you're capable." This is where we get the Middle Way in Buddhism. It's the middle between the extremes of ascetic discipline and pleasure seeking, but it's also the middle way in a more subtle sense. That is, don't desire to give up more desire than you can, and if you find that a problem, then don't desire to be successful in giving up more desire than you can. You see what's happening? Every time the student returns to the middle way, they move out of an extreme situation.

Third is nirvana—the goal of Buddhism. It's the state of liberation corresponding to what the Hindus call moksha. From the root *nivritti*, nirvana essentially means "blow out." Some people think that this refers to blowing out the flame of desire, but I think it means *breathing* out. In Indian thought, *prana*—breath—is the life principle.

You can't hold your breath and stay alive, and it becomes extremely uncomfortable to spend all your time holding on to life. If you hold on to life, you lose it. And what the devil is the point of surviving—of going on living—when life is a drag? But that's what people do—they spend enormous effort to maintain a certain standard of living, and that's a great deal of trouble. You get a nice house in the suburbs, and the first thing you do is plant a nice lawn, and then you have to get out and mow the damn thing all the time and buy expensive tools and machines, and soon you're involved too deep in mortgages to walk out in the garden and enjoy it. You spend all your time making money and paying bills—what a lot of rot! So nirvana is letting go—breathing out. See, nirvana is not annihilation. When you let your breath go, it comes back. Nirvana is not disappearing into some sort of undifferentiated void—it's a state of being let go. Nirvana is a state of consciousness—a state of being here and now in this life.

Finally, we come to the most complicated of the Four Noble Truths—marga. This word in Sanskrit means "path," and the Buddha famously taught an eightfold path for the realization of nirvana. It's easy to forget all the eight steps, so just remember that this eight-fold path has three divisions: *drishti*, *sila*, and *smriti*. In English, that's "understanding," "conduct," and "meditation." And each of these three divisions is preceded by the word *samyak*, which is usually translated as "right"—so, right understanding, right conduct, and right meditation. But this is a very bad translation. Samyak can mean "right" in certain contexts, but it has several other meanings, including "complete," "total," "all-embracing," and "middle-wayed"—that is, the center or balance point. So if we use this latter translation, the Buddha taught the middle-wayed way of looking at things, the middle-wayed way of understanding, the middle-wayed way of speech, and so on.

Now, this is particularly cogent when it comes to Buddhist ideas of behavior—that is, conduct. Buddhists all around the world—monks and laypeople—vow to keep the *pancha sila*: the five precepts. These aren't precepts in the sense of being commandments, however, because Buddhism doesn't offer some kind of moral law laid down by a cosmic lawgiver.

The reason one undertakes these precepts—abstaining from taking life, stealing, exploiting your sexual passions, lying and phony speech, and intoxication—is not sentimental. They don't make you into a good person. The reason one abstains from these behaviors is that it is expedient for liberation. If you go around killing people, you're going to make enemies and will have to defend yourself constantly; if you go around stealing, you're going to acquire a heap of belongings and that will also bring you enemies; if you exploit your passions, you're going to waste a lot of time on entertaining yourself; if you commit false speech, you'll get confused by taking words too seriously; and if you get intoxicated, you'll see everything through a haze, and that's not exactly awakening. In other words, the precepts are all quite practical.

Then there's smriti or samadhi—meditation. It also means recollection, memory, or present mindedness, which is funny—the same word can mean recollection and present mindedness. It means to have complete presence of mind. There's a wonderful meditation that the southern Buddhists practice that I call The House that Jack Built Meditation. You walk and say to yourself, "There is lifting of the foot, there is lifting of the foot," and then you say to yourself, "There is perception of lifting of the foot," and then, "There is a tendency toward the perception of the feeling of the lifting of the foot," and finally, "There is a consciousness of the tendency of the perception of the feeling of the lifting of the foot." So with everything you do, you know that you do it—you're self-aware. This is tricky, of course—it's not easy to do. And you will find that there are so many things to be aware of at any given moment in what you're doing that at best you can only pick out one or two of them. And when you practice this meditation, you discover that there isn't any way to actually be absentminded—all thoughts are in the present and of the present. When you discover that, you approach samadhi. Among all the sects of Buddhist and Hindus, you'll find different ideas of what samadhi is. Some people think of it as a trance, some call it a state of consciousness with no content—that is, knowing with no object of knowledge—some say it's the unification of the knower and the known. But the samadhi of which the Buddha spoke is the gateway to nirvana—it's the state in which the illusion of the ego as a separate thing disintegrates.

Then there's drishti—the middle-wayed understanding. Basically speaking, the anatman is applied in Buddhism not only to the individual ego, but also to the notion that there is a self in the universe. This is why it is generally supposed that Buddhism is atheistic, and that's true—depending on what you mean by "atheism." Common atheism positively denies the existence of any god. Well, Buddhism doesn't do that. Buddhism does not deny the Self with a capital S—the great atman or whatnot. What it says is that if you make conceptions and doctrines about these things, you're liable to become attached to them, and you'll therefore start believing instead of *knowing*. Remember there's a saying in Zen: "Buddhism is a finger pointing at the moon—don't mistake the finger for the moon." And as we might say in the West, "The idea of God is a finger pointing at God," but most people don't follow the finger—instead they suck it for comfort.

The Buddha chopped off the finger and undermined all metaphysical beliefs. There are multiple dialogues in the Pali scriptures in which people try to corner the Buddha into a metaphysical position: "Is the world eternal?" The Buddha didn't answer. "Is the world not eternal?" The Buddha answered not. "Is the world both eternal and not eternal?" Nothing. "Is the world neither eternal or not eternal?" More nothing. Throughout it all, the Buddha maintained what's called *the noble silence* or *the thunder of silence*, because his silence was not a void. It was an open window through which we can see—not concepts or ideas or beliefs, but the very goods. If you say what it is that you see, you erect an image and an idol, and you misdirect people. So it's better to destroy people's beliefs than to give them beliefs. I know it hurts, but it's true. It's what cracks the eggshell and lets out the chick.

This is why the truth is not told directly in Buddhism, but suggested or indicated in dialogue form. A method of interchange occurs between teacher and student whereby the teacher constantly pricks the student's bubbles. That's what it's all about. And because that's the way it is, we find that Buddhism changes over time—it develops and grows as people make explorations from the Buddha's suggestions. People find out all kinds of new things—they explore the mind and all of its tricks. Then they talk about these things and teach them to others. So any idea that you can get back to the simple, original teachings of the Buddha is misleading—you don't *get back* to Buddha, you can only *go on* to Buddha. Like an acorn, Buddhism is a living tradition that grows and grows. After the tree starts to grow, you don't try to go back to the original acorn—you grab a brand new acorn and that becomes the seed for another tree.

Let me warn you: the scholarly study of Buddhism is a magnum opus beyond belief. There are endless canonical scriptures in Pali and Sanskrit and Tibetan and Chinese, and most of these scriptures are unbelievably boring. They were written by monks with plenty of time to pass on wet afternoons during the monsoon season, and they repeat and elaborate and present all kinds of fanfare. For example, they might introduce and describe any number of Buddhas and beings—how they assembled and how they sat and what kind of bows they made and all this jazz. Then, finally, there might be a few pearls of wisdom dropped by the Buddha in there somewhere. So you've been warned. It's all right to read the *Dhammapada* or the *Diamond Sutra* or the *Lankavatara*, but when you get mixed up with the larger *Prajnaparamita* and all those things, you're in deep water.

Also keep in mind that Buddhists are funny about scriptures—they don't treat them the way that Christians treat the Bible. Buddhists respect their scriptures—they might even occasionally read them. But mostly, they feel that the written word is purely incidental. It's not the point. In fact, it can be a very serious obstacle. As Chuang Tzu, the Taoist sage, once said, "Just as a dog is not considered a good dog just for being a good barker, a man is not considered a good man just for being a good talker." So we have to watch out for the traps of words.

16

Impermanence by Any Name

One of the fundamental points of Buddhism is that the world is in flux. The Buddha emphasized impermanence, the unreality of a permanent self, and suffering. Really, suffering arises from a person's failure to accept the other two characteristics—change and lack of permanent self. I meet you today and I see you again tomorrow, and you look pretty much as you looked yesterday, so I think that you're the same person—but you aren't. Not really. When I watch a whirlpool, that whirlpool never really holds any water—the water is all the time rushing through it. In the same way, a university—what is a university? The students come and go, the faculty come and go at a somewhat slower rate, the buildings change, the administration changes—what stays the same? So a person, a whirlpool, and a university are all patterns—doings of particular kinds. Every one of us is a whirlpool in the tide of existence. Every cell in our body—every molecule, every atom—is in constant flux. Nothing can be pinned down. Our observation of atomic and subatomic particles modifies their behavior—what are they doing when we're not looking at them? Does the light in the refrigerator really go off when we close the door?

So Buddhist philosophy is a philosophy of change. From one point of view, change is just too bad. Everything flows away, and there's a kind of sadness to that—a kind of nostalgia, maybe even rage.

And there must be some resistance to change in order for there to be this wonderful manifestation of form. That's the dance of life. But the human mind is terribly aware of time, so we think a great deal about the future, and we know on some level that every visible form is going to disappear and be replaced by so-called others. But are these others actually "others"? Or are they the same forms returning? That's a great puzzle. Are next year's leaves on that tree the same as this year's leaves? What would we mean by "the same"? They'll be the same shape, they'll have the same botanical characteristics, but you'll be able to pick up a shriveled leaf from last autumn and note the difference between the two. In that sense, they are not the same. What happens when a musician plays a certain piece of music today and then the same piece tomorrow? Is it the same piece of music, or another? There's a Pali phrase for this: *nacha so, nacha anno*. It means "not the same and yet not another."

In this way, Buddhism talks about reincarnation without having to believe in some kind of soul entity that is reincarnated—some kind of atman or fixed self that moves from one life to another. And this is true in our lives as they go on now, from moment to moment, as it would be true of our lives as they appear and reappear again over millions of years—it doesn't make the slightest difference. There are long intervals and short intervals, high vibrations and low vibrations. When you hear a high note in the musical scale, you can't hear any holes in it—it goes too fast and it sounds completely continuous. But when you hear the lowest audible notes, you can feel the shaking—that's the music going on and off. In the same way, as we live now from day to day, we experience ourselves living at a high rate of vibration, and we appear to be continuous because we don't notice the gaps. But the rhythm that runs from generation to generation and from life to life is much slower, so we notice the gaps. So we live on many different levels of rhythm.

This is the nature of change. If you resist it, you have dukkha. You have frustration and suffering. But on the other hand, if you understand change, you don't cling to it and you let it flow. Then it's no problem—it becomes positively beautiful. That's why in poetry the theme of the evanescence of the world is beautiful. Percy Bysshe Shelley writes:

> *The One remains, the many change and pass*;
> Heaven's light forever shines, *Earth's shadows fly*;
> Life, *like a dome of many-coloured glass*,
> Stains the white radiance of Eternity,
> Until Death tramples it to fragments . . .

What's beautiful in that? Is it that heaven's light shines forever? Or is it rather the dome of many-colored glass that shatters? See, it's always the image of change that really makes a poem. And the speaker is aware of the fact that things are always running out, that things are always disappearing, and this has some hidden marvel in it. The Japanese word *yugen* refers to subtle profundity, but it's also a way of digging change. It's described poetically—you feel yugen when you see, out in the distance, some ships hidden behind a far-off island. You feel yugen when you watch wild geese fly, then suddenly disappear in the clouds. You feel yugen when you look across at a mountain you've never been to before, and you see the sky on the other side. You don't go over there to look and see what's on the other side—that wouldn't be yugen. You let the other side be the other side, and it invokes something in your imagination, but you don't attempt to define it or pin it down.

In the same way, the coming and going of things in the world is marvelous. They go, but where do they go? Don't answer—that would spoil the mystery. Things vanish into the mystery. And if you try to pursue them, you destroy yugen. There's a Chinese poem that says, "The wind drops, but the petals keep falling. The bird calls, and the mountain becomes more mysterious." Isn't that strange? There's no wind anymore, yet petals are dropping and the bird in the canyon cries, and that one sound in the mountains brings out the silence with a wallop. Slight impermanences bring out change, and they give you this very strange sense—yugen, the mystery of change.

Suppose that by some kind of diabolical magic I could make you stay the same age forever. It would be awful. In a thousand years, you'd be a beautiful hag. The trouble is that we have one-sided minds—we only notice the wave of life when it is at its peak or crest. We don't notice it when it's at the trough—not in the ordinary way. For us, it's the peak that counts. Think about a buzz saw. It seems that the tips of the teeth are the things that do the cutting, not the valleys between the teeth. But you can't have any tips without those valleys—the saw can't cut without tips *and* valleys. And we ignore that. We don't notice the valleys as much as we notice the mountains. Valleys point down, mountains point up, and we prefer things that point up because up is good and down is bad. So since we ignore the valley aspect of things, all wisdom begins by emphasizing the valley aspect as distinct from the peak, and looking at the valleys makes us very uncomfortable. We want to get pleasure by just looking at the peaks, but this actually denies us pleasure, because secretly we know that every peak is followed by a valley—*the valley of the shadow of death*. And we are always afraid because we are not used to looking at valleys—we're not used to living *with* them. They represent to us the strange and threatening unknown. Maybe we're afraid that the valleys will overwhelm and conquer the peaks. Maybe death is stronger than life. Life always seems to require so much effort, whereas death is something into which you slide effortlessly.

So we resist change, ignorant of the fact that change is life, ignorant of the fact that nothing is invariably the adverse face of something. Most people are afraid of space. They ignore space and think of it as nothing. But space and solid are two ways of talking about the same thing, which is space/solid. You'll never find space without solids, and you'll never find solids without space. There can't be a universe in which there is only space—space between what? Space is relationship. Space always goes with solid, like back goes with front. But the divisive mind ignores space and thinks it's the solids that do everything—that solid is the only thing that's real. In other words, conscious attention ignores intervals. But consider music. What you really hear when you hear a melody is the interval between one tone and another—the steps, as it were, on the scale. So it's the interval that's important. In the same way, the intervals between this year's leaves and last year's leaves—or this generation of people and the last generation of people—are just as important. Actually, you can't say that either the intervals or what's between the intervals is more important than the other, because they go together. Space, night, death, darkness . . . *not being there* is an essential component of *being there*. You can't have one without the other.

In the strictest Buddhist terms, the follower of the way of Buddha seeks deliverance from attachment to the world of change. The Buddha described nirvana—the state beyond change—as "the unborn, the unoriginated, the uncreated, the unformed." But when someone seeks nirvana as a state different from samsara, they are actually seeking something permanent. So over time, the Buddhists thought about this a great deal, which is how there came to be this split between the two great schools—the Theravada (sometimes disrespectfully known as the Hinayana) and the Mahayana. *Yana* means "vehicle," "conveyance," "diligence," or "ferryboat." *Hina* means "little," and *maha* means "great," so you have the little vehicle and the great vehicle. So what's going on here? The Mahayanists came along and said, "Your little vehicle just gets a few people who are very tough ascetics across to the other side to nirvana, whereas our great vehicle shows people that nirvana is not different from ordinary life." So when you reach nirvana, if you think you have actually attained nirvana—that you have caught the secret of the universe and succeeded and attained peace—that's only a false peace. You've become a stone Buddha—you have a new illusion of the changeless. So they call that kind of person a *Pratyekabuddha*—a private Buddha who has it all to themselves.

In contrast to a Pratyekabuddha—who gains nirvana and stays there—the Mahayanists present the idea of the bodhisattva, a kind of junior Buddha who has reached nirvana and chosen to return to everyday life to deliver all other beings. They're a kind of savior figure. In the popular Buddhism of Tibet, China, and Japan, people worship the bodhisattvas, particularly those like Kuan Yin—called Kannon in Japan.

So people revere these bodhisattvas as saviors who've come back to save everyone, but there's a more esoteric interpretation of this. The bodhisattva "returning to the world" means that they have discovered that you don't have to go anywhere to find nirvana—nirvana is where you are, provided you don't object to it.

Everything is change. Nothing can be held on to. And if you go with the flux, you flow with it. However, if you resist the stream, it fights you. If you realize this, you swim with the flow—you go with it, and you're at peace. This is particularly true when it comes to those moments when life really seems to be taking us away, and the stream of change is going to swallow us completely. And so at the moment of death, we withdraw and say, "No, no, no! Not that! Not yet!" But the whole problem is that we don't realize that the only thing to do when that moment comes is to go over the waterfall—just as you go on from one day to the next, just as you go to sleep at night. When the moment comes, we should be absolutely willing to die.

I'm not preaching. I'm not saying that you *should* be willing to die in the sense that you should muscle up your courage and put on a good front when the terrible event finally arrives. That's not what I'm saying at all. What I'm saying is that you can only die well if you understand this system of waves, if you understand that your disappearance as the form in which you think you are *you*—your disappearance as this particular organism—is simply seasonal. You are as much the dark space beyond death as you are the light interval called life. These are just two sides of you—you are the total wave. Just as you can't have half a wave, you can't have half a human being—that is, someone who is born and doesn't die. That would only be half a thing.

When you don't resist change—I mean *over*resist; I'm not advocating being flabby—you see that the changing world is no different from nirvana. Remember that nirvana means "breathe out"—to let go of the breath. In the same way, we let go of the world—we don't resist change. It's all the same principle. And so the bodhisattva saves beings not by preaching sermons at them, but by showing them that they are already delivered. They are liberated by the very fact of not being able to stop changing.

You can't hang on to yourself. And you don't have to try *not* to hang on to yourself—it can't be done. That is salvation.

Memento mori—be mindful of death. G.I. Gurdjieff taught that the most important thing for anyone to realize is that you and every person you see will soon be dead. Well, that sounds so gloomy to us. We have devised a culture that fundamentally resists death. Death in the Western world is viewed as a real problem—we hush it up and pretend it hasn't happened. When you get terminal cancer and go to the hospital, all your friends come around and tell you that you're looking better, that you'll be home before you know it, and so on. And the doctors and nurses are perfectly pleasant and distant, because they know you're dying and they mustn't tell you. And when death is a problem like this, when you're dying you're not behaving right—you're supposed to live. So we don't know what to do with a dying person. But we could do otherwise. We could get around that person and say, "Listen, man—I have great news for you! You're going to die, and it's going to be great. No more bills, no more responsibilities, no worries. You're going to just die, so let's go out with a bang. We'll throw a big party, put some morphine in you so you don't hurt so much, prop you up in bed, and bring all your friends around. We're going to have champagne, and you'll die at the end of the party, and it's just going to be marvelous!"

So let's try on some new thinking: death is a healthy, natural event like being born. And a little change in social attitude about this will fortify everybody. We should congratulate those about to die, because the time just before you die is a wonderful opportunity for liberation. Death isn't terrible—it's just going to be the end of you as a system of memories. So you've got a great chance right before it happens to let go of everything, because you know it's all going to go, and knowing that will help you let go. You can give your possessions away and say what you need to say—I mean, if there's something you're hanging on to and it's bothering you, then say it. I don't mean necessarily a last confession, just anything that you need to say before you go. When the moment comes, the main thing is your attitude, and death could be as positive as birth and should be a matter for rejoicing. So if we're going to have a good religion around, this is one of the places where it can start. And we should have something like an Institute for Creative Dying, in which you can either choose a champagne cocktail party, or partake in glorious religious rituals and priests and things like that, or take psychedelic drugs, or listen to special kinds of music, or just about anything. And all these arrangements will be provided for in a hospital for delightful dying. That's the thing—to go out with a bang instead of a whimper.

17

The Doctrine of Emptiness

When you discover that there is nothing to cling to and that there isn't anybody to cling to them, everything is quite different. It becomes amazing. Not only do all your senses become more wide-awake and you feel almost that you are walking on air, but you also finally see that there's no duality—there's no difference between the ordinary world and nirvana. They're the same world, and the only difference between them is a point of view.

Of course, if you keep identifying yourself with some sort of stable entity that sits and watches the world go by, if you don't acknowledge your union, if you don't recognize your inseparability from everything else that there is, if you insist on trying to take a permanent stand—on trying to be a permanent witness of the flux—then it will grate against you, and you will feel very uncomfortable. It's a fundamental feeling in most of us that we are witnesses. We feel that behind the stream of our thoughts, feelings, and experiences there is something that is the thinker, feeler, and experiencer. And this thing belongs within and not outside the changing panorama of experience.

This is what you could call a "cue signal." At one point, when someone wanted to record your telephone conversation, it was ruled that there should be a beep every seventy seconds in order to cue you in that the conversation was being recorded. In a similar way, in our everyday experience, there is a beep that tells us that we're having a continuous experience. It's like when a composer arranges some music, and they keep it in a recurrent theme but make several variations off that theme. There isn't a constant noise going all the way through to tell you that the piece is continuous, although there is such a thing in Hindu music—the drone. And that drone represents the eternal self behind all the changing forms of nature, but that's only a symbol. To find out what is eternal, you can't make an image of it—you can't hold on to it.

It's psychologically more conducive to liberation to remember that the thinker or the feeler or the experiencer and the experiences are all together—they're all one. However, if out of anxiety you try to stabilize or keep permanent some kind of separate observer, then you're in for conflict. This sense of a separate observer—a thinker of the thoughts—is an abstraction we create out of memory. We think of the self—the ego, rather—as a repository of memories, a kind of safety deposit box or filing cabinet place where all our experiences are stored. But that's not a very good idea. It's more that memory is a dynamic system—it's a repetition of rhythms, and these rhythms are all part and parcel of the ongoing flow of present experience. How do you distinguish between a memory and something known in the moment? Actually, you don't know anything at all unless you remember it, because if something happens that is purely instantaneous—a flash of light lasting only one millionth of a second, for example—you don't really experience it. It doesn't give you enough time to remember it, so it doesn't make an impression. All present knowledge is memory.

You look at something, and the rods and cones in your retina jiggle around and set up a series of vibrations or echoes in your brain, and these echoes keep reverberating. The brain is incredibly complicated. For example, everything you know is remembered, but there is a way in which we distinguish between seeing somebody here now and the memory of having seen somebody else who is not here now, but whom you did see in the past. And you know perfectly well when you remember that other person's face that it's not an experience of the person being here. How is this? Well, memory signals have a different cue attached to them than present time signals—they carry a different vibration. But sometimes the wiring gets mixed up, and present experiences come to us with a memory cue attached to them, which is when we experience déjà vu. We feel quite sure that we've experienced this thing before.

We don't ordinarily recognize that, although memories are a series of signals with a special kind of cue attached to them so that we don't confuse them with present experiences, they are actually part of the present moment experience. They are part of this constantly flowing life process, and there is no separate witness standing aside from the process, watching it all go by. And you can accept that and no longer clutch to this sense of a separate self. And that's why death should be an occasion for great celebration—it's the opportunity for the greatest of all experiences when you finally let go, and you can do that when you know there's nothing else to do.

So in Buddhist philosophy, this acceptance of change is the doctrine of the world as the void. This teaching did not emerge prominently until well after the Buddha died—we only begin to see it really emerge around 100 BCE, and it didn't reach its peak until 200 CE. The doctrine was formed by Mahayana Buddhists, who developed a whole class of literature called the Prajnaparamita. *Prajna* means "wisdom" and *paramita* can be translated as "for crossing over" or "for going beyond." Versions of the Prajnaparamita are recited by Buddhists all over the world, particularly a short version called The Heart Sutra, and the text contains the phrase, "Form is emptiness, emptiness is form," and then goes on to elaborate on this theme. So it was supposed by early missionaries that Buddhists are nihilists—that Buddhists assert that the world is really nothing—but the philosophy is far more subtle than that.

The main person who propagated these teachings was Nagarjuna, who lived somewhere around 200 CE. He possessed one of the most astonishing minds that the human race has ever produced. The name of Nagarjuna's school of thought is called *Madhyamaka*, which means "the doctrine of the Middle Way" or "the doctrine of emptiness."

Emptiness essentially means "transience"—nothing to grasp, nothing permanent—and it specifically refers to ideas of reality, meaning that reality escapes all concepts. If you say, "There is a God," that's a concept. If you say, "There is no God," that's also a concept. And so Nagarjuna emphasized the dialectic method of teaching Buddhism, specifically at the University of Nalanda, which was destroyed when the Muslims invaded India but which has been reestablished in modern times. The dialectic method is perfectly simple and can be done with an individual student and teacher or with a group—you'd be amazed at how effective it is when it involves precious little more than discussion. The teacher gradually elicits from participants their basic premises on life—what their fundamental assumptions are. What is right and wrong? What is the good life? Where do you take your stand? And the teacher finds this out for each student and then demolishes it.

When you lose your fundamental beliefs, you lose your personal compass. And you get frightened and immediately look for something to depend on. And in this dialectic method, the teacher doesn't offer any alternative suggestions, they just continue the process of examination: "Why do you think you have to have something to depend on?" Now, this is kept up over quite a period of time, and the only thing that keeps students from going insane is the presence of the teacher, who seems to be perfectly happy. And when students finally realize the void—emptiness—they are liberated, and yet they can't quite say why or what it is that they found out. That's why it's called the void. Nagarjuna continued on to teach that you must "void the void"—that is, you mustn't cling to the void. And so the void of nonvoid is the great state, as it were, of Nagarjuna's Buddhism. But you must remember that all that has been voided—all that has been denied—are those concepts in which one has hitherto attempted to pin down what is real. Zen teaches that "you cannot nail a peg into the sky." To be someone of the sky—to be someone of the void—means that you don't depend on anything. When you're not hung up on anything, you are the only thing that isn't hung up on anything, which is the universe, which doesn't hang. Where would it hang? It has no place to crash or fall on.

This is a strange notion to people like us who are accustomed to rich imageries of the divine—the Lord God in Heaven resplendent with glory with all the colors of the rainbow, surrounded by golden saints and angels and everything like that. And we feel that's a positive—we've got a real rip-roaring gutsy religion full of color. But it doesn't work that way. The clearer your image of God, the less powerful it is—it's more of an idol than anything. But voiding that image completely isn't going to turn it into what you think of as void. What do you think of as void? Being lost in a fog? In darkness? In something like the space behind your eyes? Some blank nothingness? None of those ideas are the void.

The sixth patriarch of Zen—Huineng—taught that it was a great mistake for people who practice meditation to try to make their minds empty. A lot of people try to do that. They sit down and try to have no thoughts whatsoever in their minds, and not only no thoughts but also no sensations. People close their eyes and plug their ears and generally go in for sensory deprivation. And that can be quite interesting—it sends some people crazy, some people it doesn't bother at all, and some people get a pleasant sensation of weightlessness. I've said elsewhere that the person who really accepts transience begins to feel weightless. When D.T. Suzuki was asked what it is like to experience satori—enlightenment—he replied, "It's like everyday experience—but about two inches off the ground." And Chuang Tzu once said, "It's easy enough to stand still—the difficulty is walking without touching the ground."

Why do we feel so heavy? It's not just a matter of gravity or weight—we feel that we carry these bodies around. As the Zen koan asks, "Who is it that carries this corpse around?" In common speech, we talk about life being a *drag* or *laying our burden down*. Who is carrying the burden? That's the question. And when there's nobody left for whom the body can be a burden, the body is no longer a burden. But as long as you fight it, it's a burden. And when there's nobody left to resist the thing we call change (which is simply another word for life), when we dispel the illusion that we think our thoughts instead of being just a stream of thoughts, when we lose the notion that we feel our feelings instead of being just feelings, then life is no longer a burden. Feeling feelings is a redundant expression, like saying that you hear sounds when hearing *is* sound—there are no sounds that are not heard. Seeing *is* sight—you don't *see sights*. That's ridiculous.

When we think redundantly like this, it's comparable to oscillation in an electrical system where there's too much feedback. On old-fashioned telephones, the receiver and the mouthpiece were separate, and if you really wanted to annoy someone, you would put the receiver to the mouthpiece and create this terrible howl that could be very hard on the ears. That's due to the oscillation. So when you get to thinking that you think you thoughts, there's a similar consequence—"I am worried and I ought not to worry, but because I can't stop worrying, I'm worried because I worry." You see where this leads? For us, that oscillation means anxiety. But Nagarjuna's method abolishes anxiety, because you discover that no amount of anxiety makes any difference to anything that's going to happen. It doesn't matter what you do—you're going to die. Don't put that off in the back of your mind as something to consider later—it's the most important thing to consider right now, because it enables you to let go. So you don't have to defend yourself all the time. You don't have to waste all your energy on self-defense.

In Buddhist imagery, the void is often symbolized by a mirror. A mirror has no color to it—it merely reflects all colors that appear in it. Huineng also said that the void was like space. Space contains everything—mountains, oceans, stars, good people, bad people, plants, animals, everything. And the mind is like that. Space *is* your mind. It's difficult for us to see that because we think we're *in* space and that we look out *at* it. All space, all types of space—visual, dimensional, audible, temporal, musical, tangible—are the mind. They're dimensions of consciousness. And so the great space that every one of us apprehends from a slightly different point of view in which the universe moves—is the mind. So the mind is represented as a mirror, because the mirror has no color in it, yet it's able to receive all the different colors. Thirteenth-century Christian mystic Meister

Eckhart said, "In order to see color, my eye has to be free from color." In the same way, in order to see, hear, think, and feel, you have to have an empty head. The reason why you're not aware of your brain cells is that they're void, and for that reason, you are able to experience.

So that's the central principle of Mahayana. When the Hindu Buddhist monks went to China, and the Chinese saw them trying to sit perfectly still and not engage in any worldly activities—and these monks were celibate—the Chinese thought they were crazy. Why do all of that? The Chinese were very practical, so they reformed Buddhism and allowed Buddhist priests to marry. And their favorite story from India was about a layman—the wealthy merchant Vimalakirti—who could out-argue any other disciple of the Buddha. He even won a debate against the bodhisattva of wisdom, Manjushri. They all had a contest to define the void. The monks gave their definitions, and Manjushri gave his, and then it was Vimalakirti's turn. Well, the businessman said nothing. And that's how he won the whole contest. The thunder of silence.

About the Author

Alan Watts was born near London in 1915. From a young age, he lived with Far Eastern images from a large collection of Chinese and Japanese art kept by his mother, a boarding school teacher for children of missionaries to Asia. He soon expressed an interest in Eastern philosophy and, while still a schoolboy, declared himself a Buddhist after discovering the Buddhist Lodge in London, where he met author Christmas Humphreys and later D. T. Suzuki. Watts became editor of the Lodge's journal, *The Middle Way*, and wrote his first booklet at the age of sixteen. In the late thirties, he moved from London to New York and, a few years later, received a master's degree in theology from Seabury-Western Seminary near Chicago, and became an Episcopalian minister for six years before leaving the church in 1950 and moving to San Francisco in 1951. There, at the invitation of Frederic Spiegelberg, he taught at the American Academy of Asian Studies. Subsequently he became dean of the academy, and in 1957 published *The Way of Zen*—one of the first bestselling books on Buddhism. In 1958, he set out on the first of what would be many national and international lecture tours, speaking at colleges, universities, and later at emerging growth centers. He was eventually awarded an honorary doctorate of divinity from the University of Vermont and earned a fellowship from Harvard University. By the midsixties, Watts had become the West's foremost interpreter of Buddhism, Zen, Hinduism, and Taoism.

Alan Watts is the author of more than twenty-five books, including *The Book: On the Taboo Against Knowing Who You Are*, *The Wisdom of Insecurity*, and *Psychotherapy East and West*. After leaving the American

Academy of Asian Studies, he continued to write and travel throughout the sixties and early seventies, and recorded hundreds of interviews, lectures, seminars, as well as two television series. He wrote for *Elle*, *Playboy*, *Redbook*, and the *Chicago Review*, and was adopted as a spiritual figurehead by advocates of the counterculture. He died at his home near the Muir Woods in 1973. His son, Mark Watts, carries on his father's work through the Alan Watts Electronic University, and has published courses and radio series from the extensive Alan Watts audiovisual archives, as well as having produced the documentary film *Why Not Now?*

About Sounds True

Sounds True is a multimedia publisher whose mission is to inspire and support personal transformation and spiritual awakening. Founded in 1985 and located in Boulder, Colorado, we work with many of the leading spiritual teachers, thinkers, healers, and visionary artists of our time. We strive with every title to preserve the essential "living wisdom" of the author or artist. It is our goal to create products that not only provide information to a reader or listener, but that also embody the quality of a wisdom transmission.

For those seeking genuine transformation, Sounds True is your trusted partner. At SoundsTrue.com you will find a wealth of free resources to support your journey, including exclusive weekly audio interviews, free downloads, interactive learning tools, and other special savings on all our titles.

To learn more, please visit SoundsTrue.com/freegifts or call us toll-free at 800.333.9185.